FEEDING YOUR PET
BIRD

with 80 Photographs

Petra M. Burgmann, DVM

Illustrations by
Michele Earle-Bri

D1042670

BARRON'S

All inquiries should be addressed to:
Barron's Educational Series, Inc.
250 Wireless Boulevard
Hauppauge, New York 11788

International Standard Book No. 0-8120-1521-5

Library of Congress Catalog Card No. 93-25246

Library of Congress Cataloging-in-Publication Data

Burgmann, Petra M.
    Feeding your pet bird / Petra M. Burgmann ; illustrations by
    Michele Earle-Bridges.
      p.   cm.
    Includes bibliographical references (p.) and index.
    ISBN 0-8120-1521-5
          1. Cage birds—Nutrition. 2. Cage birds—Feeding
        and feeds. I. Title.
        SF463.5.B87   1993   93-25246
        636.6'8—dc20   CIP

PRINTED IN HONG KONG

3456   9927   987654321

Contents

About the Author

Petra Burgmann, who received her Bachelor of Science and Doctor of Veterinary Medicine degrees from the University of Guelph, has been practicing exotic pet medicine since 1984. She is the author of numerous articles and has contributed chapters to several veterinary texts. Dr. Burgmann serves as veterinary consultant for the Ontario Science Centre and is a regular guest lecturer in exotic pet medicine at the University of Guelph. She has been a guest on CFRB and CBC radio, as well as on "The Monitor" television program.

Preface

My desire to write this book arose from my own frustration with the lack of integrated knowledge regarding pet avian nutrition. My feeling was that if I as an avian practitioner felt overwhelmed and unclear about the information I was being supplied, no doubt others felt the same. This book is an attempt to gather together the best of the currently available literature and present it in a form that is more readily accessible for pet owners, aviculturists, and other avian practitioners.

Pet avian nutrition is a rapidly changing field, and no doubt research that is now underway will result in changes in the information presented here. It is my hope that this book will help to clarify some of the issues that are of current interest, and act as a springboard for further research and discussion.

The author wishes to thank all of the people who helped to put this book together. Of special note are: Judy McFarlen, my associate, who first suggested the book be written; Christa Burgmann, who was patient enough to read the first cumbersome draft and who always provided loving support; Rick Axelson, who was kind enough to spend hours helping me with photographs; Dean Axelson, Rick Axelson, Louise Bauck, Susan Green, Mark Hagen, and B. Everett Webb who all provided wonderful photographs; Gloria Allen, Greg Harrison, Blake Hawley, Daniel Hopkins, Cheryl Lake, Mike Massie, Mark Subramanyam, Mike Underwood, and especially Mark Hagen, Tom Roudybush, Richard Topper, and Matthew Vriends, who were kind enough to share their knowledge; in memory of Samantha McKenzie who first introduced me to the people at Barron's; Barron's for their support of this project; and my staff who helped hold down the fort while I took time to write this book. Very special thanks go to my husband Donald Dawson, without whose help, support, and encouragement this book would never have been written; truly the "wind beneath my wings."

Petra Burgmann
Summer, 1993

ix

Chapter 1
The Importance of Nutrition

What Is Proper Nutrition?

When beginning a discussion of nutrition, the first essential question is: "What constitutes a proper balanced diet for pet birds?" The answer is that this question is far more complex than it initially appears. We do know that birds require the same food elements as other animals, namely proteins, fats, carbohydrates, vitamins, minerals, and water. However, what we have also discovered is that each species has different requirements in terms of which and how much of each of these elements are needed. These requirements vary not only with each group of birds—including the obvious differences one would expect from carnivorous birds, such as raptors, to herbivorous birds, such as lories and lorikeets—but also between each individual species. We are now beginning to realize that there are major differences in requirements between such species as African gray parrots and macaws.

These revelations have spawned an entire new field of research in an effort to define the requirements of each individual species, and, as yet, much remains unknown. This book, then, is not intended to provide a definitive answer to what constitutes a proper diet for all pet birds. However, what it will do is define the parameters of proper nutrition, summarize what is known about various species requirements, provide suggestions on how to make use of this knowledge, and try to collect the bewildering array of information into an easy reference guide for pet owners, bird breeders, and avian veterinarians.

Diets in the Wild

A flock of Amazons flies high above the Amazon rainforest. They are attracted by the bright color of a fruit visible in the trees below them, and they fly down to investigate. Raucous calls and chatter ring out in the forest as they grab branches

Diets for birds in the wild are as varied as their natural habitats. Each species has evolved to fill its particular ecological niche and make the best use of the food sources around it. Even to lump groups of birds together under the traditional headings of seed eaters, insect eaters, and fruit and nectar eaters denies the essential truth that most birds will make use of whatever food sources are abundant or available to them. Many seed eaters eat insects, particularly during the breeding season, and many insect eaters will eat seeds and fruit as part of their regular diet.

with their feet, pull the fruit toward them, and take a few bites, flinging pieces of fruit left and right as they fly from branch to branch in search of riper or more promising tidbits. An insect is discovered on one fruit, and eaten with relish.

Gray-cheeked parakeets are found congregating on the banks of the Manu River at the "Ccolpa de Guacamayas," "the lick of the macaws," as the locals call it, biting into the mineral-rich soil.

On the Pantanal of Brazil a group of hyacinth macaws are seen feeding on dried palm nuts gathered from the ground in an open pasture.

In the highland forest of Mexico's Sierra Madres, a pair of thick-billed parrots perch in the branches of a pine tree and dismantle a pine cone to get to the seeds hidden deep within.

A flock of chattering lories congregate in a flowering tree on Weda Island, consuming the nectar and pollen with their brushlike tongues, then eating the blossoms.

Diets in Captivity

Julio, the family canary, is kept in a tall round cage hung in the corner of the kitchen. He is provided with a bowl of seed from a box bought at the local grocery store, a cuttlebone that has not been changed in two years, and an occasional honey stick. He has never been out of his cage. The back of his head is bald.

Growly is a wild-caught African gray parrot. He has learned to tolerate the presence of humans and will sit on a T-stand, but his diet consists solely of sunflower seeds. The owner stopped buying seed mixes two years ago when he realized Growly was just eating the sunflower seeds anyway. Now and again the owner will offer a fruit or vegetable, but the bird just picks it up and throws it out, so the owner doesn't do it very often. The bird sneezes a lot, and occasionally falls off his perch.

Buddy, the budgie, is out of his cage most of the day. His owners offer him every treat mix on the market, honey sticks weekly, and he insists on sharing a piece of buttered toast at breakfast. He has an obesity problem and a fatty tumor on his chest.

Claudia, the cockatoo, was hand-raised, but she was weaned onto seeds and corn. Her owners want to provide a better diet, but the only thing they have been able to get her to eat is the occasional piece of orange. Her feathers are in poor condition, and she sleeps most of the day.

The different scenarios described above are no exaggeration, and the contrasts between these birds and those described in the wild need not be belabored. Essential nutrients are lacking in more than half of the diets of the pet bird population. In many of these cases these elements are not being provided due to ignorance of what the birds' needs actually are. In other cases owners are frustrated in not knowing how to change their birds' habits. Other cases are blatant examples of a refusal to take an active stewardship role in our interactions with other species on the planet, beginning with our interactions with our own pets.

Where Did We Go Wrong?

Seed feeding became popular with the reemergence of the bird as a family pet in the 1950s and 1960s. Seeds were chosen for a variety of reasons. Aside from the fact that psittacine birds were known to eat seeds in the wild, seeds were cheap, readily available, and could be stored for months at a time without spoiling.

What was ignored was that, with the exception of millet, which is eaten by wild budgies in agricultural areas, the seeds present in seed mixes are not found in the natural habitat of most of the species kept as pets.

The psychological aspects of diet selection were also ignored. To a large extent diet selection is a learned behavior, conveyed from parent to offspring, or at the very least, from bird to bird within a flock. Color, texture, taste, shape, and size also play an important role and will be discussed at length later in the book.

In the past twenty years a new appreciation for the importance of nutrition has occurred in the human population. The information has also been applied to feedstock and the pet food industry as it relates to dogs and cats. Yet when one compares what has been done in the poultry industry with what is currently being done in pet bird nutrition, it is obvious that pet bird nutrition is years behind in terms of both available information and public perception of the needs of pet birds.

The poultry industry has studied weight gains, maximum production figures, disease prevention, fat vs. protein ratios, dietary needs, and so forth, to the point that it has been able to create a highly efficient, highly specialized production machine.

There are two reasons psittacine aviculture and pet bird nutrition have fallen behind poultry management. The first is that for many of the species bred in captivity only one or two eggs are produced yearly (if the birds can be induced to breed at all), and each egg is so valuable that the exhaustive necropsy and analysis techniques that have been available for poultry are unthinkable for aviculturists. However, the second reason is one that can be rectified. Because accurate information was originally unavailable, aviculturists ended up creating their own myths and legends to increase their production rates. Two drops of wheat germ oil on Tuesdays; niger seed; conditioning food recipes of all types; aviculturists have become so caught up in their own myths that they are reluctant to change.

To give the pet food industry credit, it should be acknowledged that tremendous strides have been made in the past few years. The variety of products that have become available recently are tremendous. It is obvious that the industry is making a concerted effort to produce new and better products as the information becomes available from sources such as the research being done by various feed companies, internationally recognized aviculturists, nutritionists, zoos, and various other special interest groups. Unfortunately, however, there is still a great deal of ignorance of what a bird's needs actually are.

How Do We Fix It?

The first step in improving your bird's diet will be to develop a fundamental understanding of the basics of nutrition. The second step is understanding how these basics apply to pet birds, and to your bird in particular. The third step involves choosing a balanced diet. The final, and often most difficult step, is getting your bird to accept the new diet. Improving the diet of your pet bird will involve some work on your part, particularly in stubborn birds and in those species less commonly kept as pets. Changing a bird's diet may only take a few weeks in some cases, but it may take months in others. There is no doubt, however, that rewards in the quality of life and longevity of your pet will far outweigh the frustrations.

Chapter 2

The Building Blocks of Nutrition

One of the key frustrations in trying to understand nutrition lies in the complexity of the subject. A number of brilliant researchers have devoted their lives to this subject and still feel they lack many of the answers. The study of nutrition involves not only a knowledge of all the required food elements of diet, but how these elements interact with the body and with each other. These interactions are affected by external factors, such as temperature and light, internal factors, such as biological availability and metabolic state, and even less predictable variables, such as individual variation and state of health. There are many volumes written on this subject, and a book of this size can only attempt to point out the most important issues involved. However, certain key points are helpful in providing a basic understanding and these can be directly applied to improving your bird's nutritional state.

This section is divided into two parts. The first part identifies the required food elements, namely water, carbohydrates, fats, proteins, vitamins, and minerals, and the importance of energy. It provides a general overview and is sufficient for those who prefer a brief synopsis of the subject. The second part describes proteins, vitamins, and minerals in detail as well as their importance, signs of deficiency, and food sources. It is designed for those who wish a broader understanding of the importance of these elements in the diet.

The Importance of Energy

Energy is defined as the capacity to do work. In nutritional use, it refers to the capacity to keep the organism functioning. Obviously, the amount of energy a bird needs in order to keep functioning varies with the amount of work the bird is doing. If the bird is not actively growing, is not repairing damaged

tissue, is not losing or gaining weight, is not producing an egg, and is performing no work such as walking or flying, it is said to be in a state of maintenance. The energy requirement for maintenance is the minimum quantity of energy needed to promote an exact body balance. It is quantitated by measuring the heat production resulting from biological oxidations (chemical reactions) in the bird's body or loss of energy from bodily excretions.

Through various experiments, scientists have determined a formula by which they can estimate the net energy required for maintenance by birds. The formula is:

$$NE_m = BMR\ (1.0\ to\ 3.0)$$
$$BMR = K_{cal}\ (BW_{Kg}{}^{0.75})\ \text{where}$$

NE_m = net energy required for maintenance

BMR = basal metabolic rate (varies one to three-fold depending on basic metabolic needs)

K = theoretical constant for the kilocalories used by a bird during a 24-hour period. This value is 78 for non-passerine birds (e.g.

parrots) and 123 for passerine birds (e.g., canaries)

cal = calories (a calorie is that amount of energy required to raise the temperature of 1 g of water 1°C)

BW = body weight

kg = kilograms

This estimate of energy requirement is a fundamental nutritional concept. Energy is the most important element in a bird's diet, in that a bird eats to meet its energy requirements. All other aspects of feeding and ration formulation are related to the energy content of the diet.

There is one exception to the basic rule of energy as the most important dietary ingredient. If the protein level of the diet is too low, the bird will eat to exceed its energy requirements in an effort to compensate for the lack of protein. This results in obesity, and is a major cause of obesity in birds on a seed-only (thus low-protein) diet.

Aside from this one exception, how much energy the feed contains will determine how much of the food is eaten. How much is eaten will determine exactly how much of each nutrient is consumed. Carbohydrates, fats, and proteins are all sources of energy.

For many years people have argued over what is the correct level of protein in the avian diet, and consumers have often based their choice of pelleted ration on the protein level of the feed. However, comparing two rations without knowing the energy level of each is like comparing apples and oranges. In order to know exactly how much protein the bird would actually consume in one day, one must know the energy level of the feed.

Proteins

Proteins vary widely in their chemical composition, physical properties, and biological functions. What all proteins do have in common is that they are formed from basic structural components called amino acids. Amino acids are organic acids that have an amino group (NH_2) added to the acid molecule. All proteins are formed from 20 amino acids. Plants are capable of synthesizing these amino acids from nonorganic nitrogen sources by combining nitrogen, hydrogen, and phosphorus from the soil with carbon and oxygen from the air. Birds can only synthesize some of these amino acids; the rest must be supplied in the diet. Those amino acids that must be supplied in the diet are known as the essential amino acids. Arginine, histidine, leucine, isoleucine, lysine, methionine, phenylalanine, threonine, tryptophan, and valine are considered essential, and glutamic acid, glycine, and proline are often added to this list because they are needed for optimal growth in chickens and therefore may also be important in pet birds.

Proteins are involved in many different biological functions. Structurally, they are components of muscle, skin, feathers, organs, and cell membranes, and form the fibrous support network of bone. Metabolically they form enzymes, hormones, and immune antibodies. They are required for almost all chemical processes in the body, including oxygen transport, water regulation, blood clotting, healing, and growth.

Determining the total protein level in a diet is not sufficient. What is more important is the biological availability of the dietary protein. Biological availability refers to how readily the protein can be digested into amino acids, absorbed, and utilized by the body to produce new proteins. The efficient utilization of absorbed amino acids to produce new proteins is related to the distribution of essential amino acids. Proteins of highest biological availability are considered those of highest biological value. Biological value is defined as the percentage of digested and absorbed nitrogen of protein that is retained in the body for productive functions. Eggs, for example, have a biological value of approximately 100. In other words, the protein they contain can be almost completely utilized by the body. Meat proteins have a biological value of 72 to 79, whereas cereal proteins have a value of only 50 to 65. Cereal proteins are often deficient in the essential amino acids lysine, methionine, and tryptophan. If a protein is of low biological value, much more of it must be consumed in order to meet daily requirements, and even then it may still not provide some essential amino acids. So for example, dry cooked beans have higher total protein content at 21 percent than eggs do at 13 percent; however, garbanzo beans are only 42 percent digestible and have protein of less biological value than that of an egg. If the amino acids are properly balanced, adult cockatiels can be maintained on 4 percent protein while cockatiel chicks may require 20 percent. Remembering to relate this to energy levels, one can see that comparing two diets solely on the basis of protein levels is highly inaccurate.

People are often unaware of the importance that animal protein can play in the diet of birds by providing certain essential amino acids. Not only do raptors eat meat, but parrots have also been observed eating carrion, snails, and dead fish. All birds on seed-only diets are invariably deficient in several essential amino acids. Amino acid deficiency results in the failure in production of some protein structure, such as enzymes, antibodies, or feathers. Growing birds have higher protein requirements, as do breeding females.

Carbohydrates

Carbohydrates function mainly as sources of heat and energy. Plants and animals synthesize many different carbohydrates, but the basic compound is glucose from which more complex compounds are synthesized. Carbohydrates are the sugars and starches, and are grouped into monosaccharides, disaccharides, and polysaccharides.

Although the fibrous husks of seeds are also a carbohydrate called cellulose, they are not generally digested by birds and therefore are not considered a good carbohydrate source. Birds obtain their energy from the more readily available carbohydrates, such as starch, which is readily digested to glucose in the small intestine and in this form can be absorbed and utilized as an energy source.

There are many different pathways of carbohydrate metabolism in the body used to produce or store energy. The most important of these are glycolysis, the citric acid cycle, the pentose phosphate pathway, glycogen formation and degradation, and interconversions among monosaccharides. These pathways are complex and need not be discussed at length, but they have been mentioned in order to clarify the roles certain nutrients play later in the book.

The liver plays a key role in the metabolism of carbohydrates, both in producing glucose from various sources as needed as an energy source and in converting glucose into forms that can be stored in the body. Because all diets provide energy, whether they are immediately available in the form of carbohydrates or whether they are converted to carbohydrates later, carbohydrates will not be discussed at greater length.

Fats

Fats, or lipids, play several important roles in avian nutrition. They are an important energy source. The gross energy value of pure fats and oils is more than twice that of sugars and starches. They act as solvents to aid in the absorption of fat-soluble vitamins, and as a source of essential fatty acids. They are also used to reduce the dustiness of feeds, improve the palatability of a diet, and aid the passage of feeds through the pelleting machines.

Lipids are defined as water-insoluble organic molecules that can be extracted from cells of plant or animal origin by solvents, such as ether. Nutritionally, the lipids that are important are the fatty acids. There are two types of fatty acids. Unsaturated, or short-chain fatty acids, are liquid at room temperature and are referred to as oils. They contain one or more pairs of carbon atoms in which a hydrogen atom has been removed and replaced with a double bond. Saturated, or long-chain fatty acids, contain no double bonds. They are solid at room temperature and are referred to as fats.

Many fatty acids are synthesized in the body. Essential fatty acids are those that cannot be synthesized in the body and must be supplied in the diet from plant sources. Linoleic and linolenic acids are essential fatty acids that are required in the diet of birds. Arachidonic acid can be synthesized from linoleic acid, but may be required if linoleic acid levels are low. Essential fatty acids are the precursors of prostaglandins. Prostaglandins have a variety of profound hormonelike effects, including lowering blood pressure, inducing smooth muscle contraction, enhancing inflammation reactions, and many other functions.

Deficiencies of essential fatty acids result in a slowed growth rate, a general unthrifty appearance, and eventually death. Because essential fatty acids are derived from plant sources, one would not generally expect them to be deficient in even a standard seed diet. For example, corn, peanut, and soybean oil all have high levels of linoleic acid. However, fats, especially oils, tend to spoil quickly because of oxidation (the chemical process in which oxygen interacts with a substance). Oxidation is catalyzed by light and metals, such as copper and iron, and accelerated by heat. Several processes are used in the food industry to try to delay or prevent oxidation reactions, including advising that food be kept in a cool, dark place, and adding antioxidants, which are substances that prevent oxidation reactions. These substances will be discussed later in the chapter on feed additives, but the principle is mentioned here to illustrate how essential fatty acids can be lost from what would be considered a ready source if adequate precautions are not taken.

Water

Water is not generally considered a nutrient, yet it is so essential to the health of a bird that it should not be neglected. Water makes up 98 percent of the molecules present in the body. A bird may lose almost all of its body fat and 50 percent of its body protein—and live, but a loss of more than one tenth of its body water may result in death. Water content is highest in newborn animals. In adults, the proportion of the body that is water varies inversely with body fat.

Water is involved in many biological functions, including being a solvent for many compounds, transporting substances to and from the cells, and regulating body temperature of birds by evaporative cooling through the respiratory tract.

Water may be obtained by drinking, or from succulent food sources. Birds are less dependent than mammals on drinking water because they eliminate their nitrogenous wastes in the form of insoluble uric acid, which is in a more concentrated form and is less toxic than mammalian urea. Budgerigars seem most able to tolerate low water intake, but small sparrows, finches, and canaries that live mainly on diets of dry seeds do depend on a water supply.

Water quality is also of prime importance. Not only can excess levels of total solids, sodium chloride, and nitrates have a deleterious effect, but contaminated water sources can also harbor harmful bacteria and carcinogens.

A continuous, ready supply of fresh, clean drinking water cannot be overemphasized, even for those species that generally consume less water from drinking sources than from food sources.

Vitamins

Vitamins are organic substances that are considered metabolically essential in minute amounts in animal tissues.

They are conventionally divided into two groups. The fat-soluble group consists of vitamins A, D, E, and K. The water-soluble group consists of the B vitamins thiamine (B_1), riboflavin (B_2), nicotinic acid, pyridoxine (B_6), cyanocobalamin (B_{12}), as well as pantothenic acid, biotin and folic acid, inositol, choline, and vitamin C. Water-soluble vitamins are not stored in large amounts in the body and are therefore needed in constant supply. Because they are readily excreted, toxic overdose is uncommon. Fat-soluble vitamins can be stored in the body and used as needed. Toxic overdose can occur if excess levels of fat-soluble vitamins are administered, particularly vitamin D_3 in birds.

Some species of animals are able to synthesize certain vitamins in their tissues or they are able to utilize the vitamins produced by microorganisms in their digestive tract. Consequently, vitamin requirements vary from species to species, depending on their ability to synthesize or absorb each vitamin. There even appears to be a variability in requirements among different avian species and individuals, depending on the group's physiological makeup or the individual's health status and needs.

Vitamin deficiencies in pet birds are very common and have a number of causes. These causes include inadequate ingestion (due to poor diet or insufficient or improper supplementation), inadequate absorption from the intestine (due to diseases of the digestive system or parasites), or inadequate utilization (due to diseases of the liver, kidney, or other organ systems). Other causes include increased requirements, such as during breeding, molting, stress, or disease, or excess loss through excretion in liver, kidney, or bowel disease.

The most commonly recognized vitamin deficiencies in pet birds are a lack of vitamin A and vitamin D_3;

Chronic, low-grade vitamin, mineral, and amino acid deficiencies can result in poor health.

however, it is becoming more apparent that these two commonly recognized entities are just the tip of the iceberg; deficiencies in most of the vitamins listed above are present to a greater or lesser extent in all birds on seed-only diets.

Table 1 lists some dietary sources of vitamins and minerals, while Table 2 lists signs of deficiency that have been recognized in poultry and pet birds.

Minerals

Minerals are also essential for avian health and are often neglected in the discussion of what constitutes a good avian diet. They are essential to the structure of bone, play an important role in the transport of oxygen, the regulation of osmotic activity and blood acid-base levels, and are required for the activation of many enzyme systems.

Calcium, phosphorus, magnesium, sodium, chloride, potassium, and sulfur are considered the macrominerals, because they must be supplied in significant quantities in the diet. Of these, calcium is invariably deficient in a seed-only diet, and this deficiency has serious consequences to the health of the bird.

Manganese, iron, zinc, copper, cobalt, iodine, selenium, fluoride, chromium, molybdenum, silicon, and a few other trace elements are considered the microminerals, because they need only be supplied in minute quantities in order to meet the bird's needs.Calcium and iron deficiencies are the most commonly recognized mineral deficiencies in birds, though likely many others go unrecognized.

Fiber

Recent research on the importance of dietary fiber in humans has led to speculation regarding its role in dog and cat nutrition. The importance of fiber in pet bird nutrition has not been examined, although it is an area of interest and debate among many aviculturists. The purpose of this section is simply to define the terms involved in a discussion of fiber and its possible dietary implications.

Basically, fiber refers to poorly available, or unavailable, carbohydrate in the diet. It is that portion of carbohydrate that is very difficult to break down and use. Birds produce the enzymes necessary to break down simple sugars and starch, but lack the enzymes needed to break down fiber.

Fiber is classified as "insoluble" or "soluble." Insoluble fiber refers to things like cellulose and lignin, which are found in high concentration in fruits and vegetables. Soluble fiber refers to pectin and some plant gums, which are generally found in low concentrations in most foods, with the exception of oat fiber, which contains significant amounts.

The beneficial effects fiber has in the human diet relate mostly to its action in the colon, or large intestine; because parrots have such a short segment of large intestine, it is unlikely that increased dietary fiber would have much of an effect in this area. However, some other findings may apply. In humans, the presence of fiber in the diet has been found to decrease the amount of digestible carbohydrate that is available, and lower the absorption level of sugars. Soluble fiber decreases blood cholesterol levels (the reason for the present push of oat fiber in human nutrition). Fiber also tends to absorb water, thus increasing the bulkiness of the stool. In large herbivores, such as cattle, fiber plays an important role in the prevention of gastrointestinal tract ulceration. It is possible that some, if not all, of these findings may also be important in avian nutrition. Fiber also appears to alter fat and protein metabolism in some way. For example, in humans, diets containing higher levels of whole wheat bran increase fecal fat excretion, and may inhibit the activity of trypsin and chymotrypsin, two enzymes involved in protein metabolism. Whether these effects are permanent, or whether they are transient and are compensated for over time by the bowel, has not yet been determined.

It is clear, then, that fiber is not an inert substance as was once believed, but does indeed play a significant role in metabolism. The importance of its role in pet avian nutrition, however, has yet to be determined.

Grit

Traditionally, grit was believed to be essential for pet birds to aid in the mechanical grinding of food in the gizzard. However, it has since been shown that some species of pet birds can be raised on a grit-free diet and still digest their food adequately. It has also been determined that birds that are ill may ingest an excessive amount of grit, leading to impaction. This has resulted in some avian practitioners recommending that grit not be supplied in the diet.

My personal opinion lies somewhere between the two extremes. Even though grit may not be neces-

Various sizes of grit are available commercially.

sary for digestion in some species, its presence in the gizzard undoubtedly speeds the digestion of hard foods, and may indeed increase the digestibility of the diet. It has also been shown that the presence of grit in the gizzard increases the strength of the contractions of the muscular wall of the gizzard, thereby also increasing its grinding ability.

Grit can be provided in a small cup up on the side of the cage. Grit on the floor of the cage is unnecessary, and may result in the bird ingesting its own feces. No more than a few grains need be offered every few days, because grit is retained for long periods in the gizzard. This practice will also decrease the chance of impaction in an ill bird.

It is important to provide grit that is proportionate in size to the size of the bird; budgies need a much smaller grit size than parrots. There are commercial brands available in several sizes, so that obtaining the appropriate grit is seldom a problem. Charcoal-containing grits are not recommended, because charcoal has been shown to adsorb vitamins A, B_2, and K from the intestinal tract.

Chapter 3
Vitamins and Minerals in Detail

Vitamins in Detail

The Fat-Soluble Vitamins

Vitamin A: Vitamin A is necessary for normal mucoprotein synthesis, probably by helping a form of sulfur to combine with mucopolysaccharide, a building block of mucoprotein. Mucoproteins are jellylike, slippery, or sticky substances that provide lubrication or act like cement in cells. A lack of vitamin A

Orange and yellow vegetables have high vitamin A values.

makes biological membranes unstable, including those of the red blood cells. This lack also changes the structure of epithelial cells from a column to flat layers of cells full of keratin. Vitamin A's main function, then, is to protect the integrity of mucous membranes and epithelial tissues of the skin, intestine, kidney, respiratory tract, and reproductive tracts. It may also be necessary for maintaining the integrity of the adrenal cortical cells responsible for the synthesis of the hormones corticosterone, deoxycorticosterone, and progesterone. It is also involved in the retinal pigment rhodopsin. Rhodopsin is broken down and resynthesized under the stimulus of light. When vitamin A is deficient, resynthesis is poor, resulting in night blindness.

Vitamin A occurs in two forms. Retinol is the natural form of vitamin A found in animal fats and fish oils. Carotenes are the form found in foods of plant origin. Beta carotene is the most active form of carotene and is converted into vitamin A by enzymatic reactions in the intestinal mucosa and liver. Some avian practitioners are of the opinion that the beta carotenes seem to be a superior source of vitamin A for birds, and may have other beneficial effects not yet recognized. I am of the same opinion, although there is no published data yet to substantiate these impressions.

All seeds, other than yellow corn, are notorious for their low vitamin A content, and large parrots on sunflower seed-only diets invariably suffer from vitamin A deficiency. In fact, it is one of the most commonly recognized vitamin deficiencies in pet birds and will be discussed again in the chapter on diet and disease. Vitamin A is also easily oxidized, and care must be taken in how foods containing these substances are processed.

Orange and yellow vegetables and fruits have high vitamin A values because of the beta carotenes they contain. Some green, leafy vegetables also contain a lot of carotene, but their yellow color is masked by the green pigment chlorophyll.

Liver is very high in pure vitamin A; however, many experts recommend that liver should not be fed more than once a month due to the toxic substances it contains. These toxic substances occur as a result of exposure of an animal to environmental pollutants, because the liver is the organ responsible for detoxification. The longer an animal is alive, the greater its exposure to environmental toxins;

therefore the liver of a calf, for example, should be less toxic than the liver of a full-grown cow.

The supplementation of cod-liver oil in the diet of psittacines was a common practice among aviculturists, and one can see that this practice probably arose in an effort to counteract vitamin A deficiency. However, cod-liver oil may not only supply excess vitamin A, but may also contribute to the destruction of vitamin E, exacerbating vitamin A deficiency. It is estimated (though not substantiated), that vitamin A requirements are 50–100 IU per day for budgerigars, 200 IU per day for Amazons, African grays, and cockatoos, and up to 500 IU per day for large macaws.

Vitamin D_3—Cholecalciferol: Vitamin D generally refers to two chemically similar compounds: vitamin D_2, or calciferol, and vitamin D_3, or cholecalciferol. Vitamins D_2 and D_3 have about the same potency for most mammals, but vitamin D_3 is 30 to 100 times as effective as vitamin D_2 in birds. Several other compounds also have vitamin D-like

A severe case of rickets in a pigeon.

activity, but we will restrict this discussion to the most important element for birds, vitamin D_3.

Vitamin D is one of the most complex elements that will be discussed in this section. Not only must it be in the active form to be used in the body, which depends on the function of the liver and the kidney, the availability of direct sunlight, or ingestion of the vitamin in its active form, but it is also influenced by calcium, phosphorus, strontium, and magnesium, and the glands and hormones that control these minerals.

Vitamin D is ingested and absorbed from the intestine where it is transported to the liver. In the liver it is converted to relatively inactive excretion products called vitamin D esters, and into an important compound called 25-hydroxy-

Fresh walnuts can be a good source of vitamin E.

cholecalciferol. When calcium is needed, this substance undergoes another chemical process in the kidney to produce 1,25-dihydroxycholecalciferol, which is the active form of vitamin D_3. This active form enhances the absorption of calcium from the intestine by inducing a calcium-binding protein that actively transports calcium. This calcium-binding protein has been found in the intestines, kidney, and shell gland of laying hens, and in chick brain tissue. There is also evidence that vitamin D mobilizes bone mineral to help maintain serum levels of calcium and phosphorus, and plays a role in the deposition of calcium salts into the cartilaginous matrix of bone. Vitamin D may also play a direct role in phosphorus metabolism by being involved in a vitamin D-dependent active phosphate pump. It is also known to affect the release of energy within the cell.

The clinical signs of vitamin D deficiency relate to its effects on calcium and phosphorus metabolism. Rickets is the term applied to the clinical signs of vitamin D deficiency in young animals. In adults, the condition is called osteomalacia. These diseases are discussed in the chapter on diet and disease.

Vitamin D metabolism is influenced by many factors. If vitamin D_3 is not supplied in the diet, the ultraviolet rays of direct sunlight are required to convert the precursor of vitamin D (7-dehydrocholesterol), which is present in the skin, to activated vitamin D_3. (The equivalent wavelengths of ultraviolet light may be supplied by some fluorescent tubes such as Vitalites, which is why these light sources should be provided for pet birds.) Dietary strontium inhibits the synthesis of 1,25-dihydroxycholecalciferol by interfering with the kidney hydroxylase system. There also appears to be an inverse relationship between dietary vitamin D levels and serum magnesium levels.

Few foods naturally contain significant amounts of vitamin D, which is why this substance must often be supplemented in the avian diet. Fish oils are the exception, another reason why cod-liver oil has been used as a supplement in the past. However, as with vitamin A, overdosage of vitamin D_3 can have severe metabolic effects. (See Table 3, page 46.)

Vitamin E—Tocopherol: Vitamin E is not a single compound, but actually a group of compounds called tocopherols, all with similar vitamin E-like activity. Of these, alpha tocopherol has the greatest activity. There are also many synthetic chemical compounds with similar structures and a number of chemicals that are unrelated chemically to the tocopherols that also have vitamin E-like activity.

Vitamin E functions as a biological antioxidant in the cells and tissues of the body. That is, it inhibits the combining of chemical substances in the body with oxygen by combining with oxygen itself. This action protects polyunsaturated fats and other oxygen-sensitive compounds like vitamin A from being destroyed. Some oxidation reactions that occur in tissues are catalyzed by chemicals called free radicals. Free radicals are considered toxic substances because they can interact at enzyme sites or damage cell membranes. Vitamin E prevents the reactions caused by free radicals by combining with them. It also appears to have a function in maintaining the integrity of biological membranes, and protects lung cells and white blood cells from damage. Deficiency of the vitamin results in reproductive failures, muscle degeneration, degenerative lesions in the brain, liver, and heart, depression of the immune system, and some functional and/or physical damage to cell membranes.

The tocopherols are widely distributed in nature; however, they are easily destroyed by ultraviolet light and oxidizing agents. Vitamin E requirements are increased with an increase in the intake of polyunsaturated fatty acids, and in conditions that interfere with fat absorption, such as diseases of the liver or pancreas. Vitamin E deficiency may also be precipitated by excessive use of cod-liver oil, because the unsaturated fatty acids of cod-liver oil cause oxidation of vitamin E.

Vitamin K: Vitamin K consists of three chemically similar compounds known as K_1, K_2, and K_3. Vitamin K_1 is the form present in plants, and K_2 is the form produced by bacterial synthesis in the intestine. Vitamin K_3, known as menadione, is the synthetic form of the vitamin and is about twice as potent as vitamin K_1. It is water-soluble and is the form most often present in vitamin supplements.

Vitamin K is involved in the biosynthesis of the enzyme proconvertin, which is necessary for the production of prothrombin by the liver. Prothrombin is one of the chemicals involved in blood clotting. Vitamin K_1 is also involved as a coenzyme in both the electron transport and the oxidative phosphorylation systems, processes used by the body to produce energy. Vitamin K also works with vitamin D to make a protein used to help regulate blood calcium levels. Calcium is another factor important in the clotting mechanism. Clinical signs of deficiency relate to the function of vitamin K in the clotting mechanism.

Vitamin K is normally synthesized by bacterial action in the lower intestine of adult birds. However, the lower intestine is a site of poor absorption. In addition, changes in the intestinal flora caused by indiscriminate use of antibiotics, inappropriate amounts of vitamin A, or the use of mineral oil, may result in a deficiency. Young growing birds may also be deficient in this vitamin due to an underdeveloped bacterial flora.

Liver disease, which may result in decreased prothrombin formation and decreased bile secretion, can also result in vitamin K deficiency, because bile secretion is necessary for vitamin K absorption. Any disease of the intestinal tract that interferes with the absorption of fats and fat-soluble vitamins will also lead to vitamin K deficiency.

The Water-Soluble Vitamins

Vitamin B_1—Thiamine: Thiamine, like many of the B-complex vitamins, acts primarily as a biological catalyst, or coenzyme. Once absorbed from the digestive tract, it is carried to the liver, where it undergoes a chemical reaction known as phosphorylation. Phosphorylation results in the formation of two coenzymes: thiamine pyrophosphate, or cocarboxylase, and lipothiamide. Cocarboxylase acts as a coenzyme in the decarboxylation (removal of carbon dioxide) of alpha-keto acids such as pyruvic acid and alpha-ketoglutaric acid. These alpha-keto acids are part of the process of degradation of carbohydrates. Thiamine, therefore, is involved in carbohydrate metabolism, and thus, in energy metabolism in general. Energy metabolism provides energy for the body to function, and heat for the body to maintain a constant temperature. When thiamine is lacking, pyruvic acid (or its derivative, lactic acid) accumulates in the tissues causing damage. Thiamine is also involved in the synthesis of fats, protein metabolism, and the normal functioning of the nervous system. Thiamine deficiency especially affects the functions of the nervous system, the heart, and the gastrointestinal system.

Thiamine is highly soluble in water and is readily destroyed by heat. Therefore it is easily destroyed by cooking and leaches out into cooking water. Steaming or microwaving vegetables can help preserve their thiamine levels. It is also the most poorly stored of the B vitamins. Although thiamine is common in nuts and grains, freshness is important; thus, old seeds or nuts may be surprisingly deficient. Thiamine requirements are related to caloric intake; more thiamine is required in high-carbohydrate diets than in high-fat diets. Its utilization or availability can also be reduced by the presence in the diet of interfering or antagonistic compounds. An enzyme called thiaminase, present in raw fish, clams, shrimp, bracken fern, and certain bacteria, breaks down thiamine. Another compound, called pyrithiamine, competes with thiamine in the formation of cocarboxylase and thus antagonizes its function.

Vitamin B$_2$—Riboflavin: Riboflavin functions biochemically in two coenzymes: flavin mononucleotide and flavin adenine dinucleotide. It is found in all tissues, with its concentration usually paralleling metabolic activity. These coenzymes function in the oxidative degradation of pyruvate and fatty acids, and in the process of electron transport. Electron transport is a chemical reaction in which hydrogen ions (protons) and electrons from one substrate are transferred to another. These reactions are part of the carbohydrate, protein, and fat metabolism systems.

Riboflavin is easily destroyed by light. Dietary requirements appear to be related to caloric requirements and muscular activity, and are affected by heredity, growth, environment, age, and health. Evidence in animals suggests there is an increased need for riboflavin in low-protein diets because of a decreased ability of the liver to retain the vitamin. Other evidence suggests diets high in carbohydrates require less riboflavin than diets high in fat, due to an increase in synthesis of riboflavin by intestinal bacteria. Riboflavin deficiency is known to cause feather depigmentation in baby cockatiels.

Broccoli is a good source of vitamins A, K, C, riboflavin, folic acid, and calcium.

Niacin: Niacin occurs in two forms: nicotinic acid and niacinamide. Both forms are found in foods, but nicotinic acid is changed to niacinamide in the body. Niacinamide is found in two coenzymes: niacinamide adenine dinucleotide (NAD) and niacinamide adenine dinucleotide phosphate (NADP). These two coenzymes function in a large number of dehydrogenase (transporting hydrogen) reactions, at least forty of which have been identified so far. These reactions include aerobic and anaerobic oxidation of glucose (carbohydrate metabolism), fatty acid oxidation and synthesis (lipid metabolism), conversion of vitamin A to rhodopsin (needed for night vision), and the incorporation of the high-energy phosphate bonds in ADP and ATP (the important chemicals in energy metabolism).

Many animals, including birds, are capable of synthesizing niacin from the amino acid tryptophan. However, it takes 60 mg of tryptophan to make 1 mg of niacin, and tryptophan is an amino acid already deficient in most seed diets. Corn is deficient in both niacin and tryptophan, therefore, diets high in corn that are not supplemented adequately may lead to signs of deficiency. The best sources of niacin are foods that have a high-protein content.

Vitamin B$_6$: Vitamin B$_6$ exists as three chemically related substances: pyridoxine, pyridoxamine, and pyridoxal. All three forms have similar biological activity in that all three are converted into the coenzyme pyridoxal-5-phosphate in the body. This coenzyme functions in aminotransferase reactions, a chemical reaction used by the body to synthesize amino acids from alpha-keto acids. It is involved in amino acid decarboxylation (removing carbon dioxide) reactions, and in the metabolism of sulfur-containing amino acids. It is also involved in the reaction in which the amino acid tryptophan is converted into niacin. Thus, it plays an important role in many aspects of protein metabolism, including helping to manufacture many important protein compounds, such as antibodies, hemoglobin, and hormones. Deficiency of the vitamin causes changes in the skin, in red blood cells, and in nervous system tissues.

Vitamin B$_6$ is rapidly destroyed by light in alkaline or neutral solutions. True deficiency seldom occurs naturally, because vitamin B6 is widespread in nature. Foods of plant origin are generally higher in pyridoxine, whereas foods of animal origin are higher in pyridoxamine and pyridoxal. There is some synthesis of the vitamin by bacteria in the lower intestine. It is believed that high-protein diets may increase dietary requirements, whereas high-carbohydrate diets are thought to increase the synthesis of the vitamin by intestinal bacteria.

Pantothenic Acid: In its pure form pantothenic acid is a pale yellow oil, but the sodium, potassium, and calcium salts of the vitamin are highly soluble in water. It is involved in many biochemical processes in the form of a coenzyme, called coenzyme A. Coenzyme A, and its derivative, acetyl-coenzyme A, are involved in many aspects of the metabolism of fats, proteins, and carbohydrates. It is also involved in the synthesis of steroid hormones, bile acids, cholesterol, acetylcholine, fatty acids, prostaglandins, and some amino acids. Acetylcholine is the chemical that acts at the nerve-muscle junction to stimulate muscular contraction. Bile acids aid in the absorption of certain nutrients from the digestive tract, like the fat-soluble vitamins. Prostaglandins have many effects on the body including altering blood pressure, inhibiting gastric secretion, and enhancing inflammation, thus aiding the function of the immune system.

Pantothenic acid is decomposed by hot acids or alkalis. It is present in all living cells and in all foods, so a true deficiency is considered rare, although absorption may be inhibited by parasitic or infectious digestive tract disorders. It is also produced by bacteria in the intestine, but it is unknown if this synthesis contributes much to the body's supply.

Folic Acid: Folic acid, folacin, and folate all refer to the same vitamin. Folic acid is the simplest form of the vitamin, and the one most often found in supplements. The biologically active forms of the vitamin occur as tetrahydrofolic acids, and vitamin C appears to be involved in their synthesis. Tetrahydrofolic acids are important in the synthesis of purines and pyrimidines, which are components of nucleic acids, the building blocks of DNA and RNA; in the synthesis of the methyl group of methionine; and in the metabolism of some amino acids, including glycine, serine, histidine, glutamic acid, and phenylalanine. Because it functions in the synthesis of DNA and RNA, it is important in making new cells, and is especially important in any body tissue where cell turnover is high; for example, in red blood cell production, in the intestine, and in growth and development. It is often found to work together with vitamin B_{12} in various reactions.

Folic acid deficiency can result from inadequate dietary intake, or increased metabolic need, such as

Growth increases the need for many vitamins and minerals.

in reproduction, growth, cancer, blood loss, or severe burns. Cooking destroys folacin, whereas vitamin C helps preserve folacin values. Intestinal bacteria can synthesize the vitamin, but antibiotics, such as sulfa drugs, reduce intestinal bacterial production.

Vitamin B_{12}: Vitamin B_{12}, also known as cyanocobalamin, is the only vitamin containing an inorganic element, cobalt. It is synthesized only by certain microorganisms, and is found in animal tissues as a result of intestinal bacterial synthesis or ingestion from nonplant sources. It is absorbed from the intestine with the help of a substance made in the stomach called the intrinsic factor. The intrinsic factor combines with the vitamin B_{12} that is released from food during digestion, and carries the vitamin to a lower part of the small intestine, the ileum, where it attaches itself to special receptor cells. The vitamin is then released from the carrier and enters these cells for absorption. Once absorbed into the body, vitamin B_{12} is involved in the formation of several coenzymes. These coenzymes play a role in fatty acid metabolism and amino acid biosynthesis, and in the synthesis of nucleotides, which are the building blocks of DNA and RNA. It functions in the production of myelin, a substance that covers and protects nerve fibers. It is also essential in the normal development and maturation of red blood cells, and in

hemoglobin production. Hemoglobin is the oxygen carrying pigment of red blood cells.

It has been suggested that excessive protein in the diet of grain-eating birds increases vitamin B_{12} requirements, which may produce signs of deficiency, especially in nestlings. Requirements for vitamin B_{12} are also increased in reproduction and in hyperthyroidism. It has also been found that the action of the intrinsic factor in facilitating the absorption of vitamin B_{12} is calcium dependent, so that a diet deficient in calcium may have some effect on vitamin B_{12} availability. Grains and vegetables are poor sources of the vitamin, and although bacteria in the intestine make some of the vitamin, far less than the amount needed daily is absorbed from this source. Although vitamin B_{12} is fairly well stored in the liver, it is my opinion that vitamin B_{12} deficiency may be a common, seldom recognized, disorder in pet birds that plays a role in many health problems.

Biotin: Biotin functions as a coenzyme in carbon dioxide fixation and in decarboxylation enzymes. It is also involved in the deamination (removal of amine) of some amino acids. Thus it plays a role in carbohydrate, fat, and protein metabolism.

Biotin is widespread in nature; therefore a naturally deficient diet is considered uncommon unless other factors are also involved. Biotin can be destroyed by oxidizing agents, acids, and alkalis. It can also be destroyed by oxidation in the presence of rancid fats. Raw egg white contains a substance called avidin that combines with biotin to form an indigestible complex. Cooking egg white destroys this factor, rendering it harmless. Because biotin is produced by bacteria in the intestine, the administration of sulfa drugs may promote a deficiency.

Vitamin C: Vitamin C is also known as ascorbic acid. The ability to synthesize ascorbic acid in the body appears to depend upon the presence of two enzymes, glucurono-reductase and gulono-oxidase. These enzymes are found in the liver and kidney of those species that are able to synthesize the vitamin from hexose sugars.

Vitamin C acts as a cofactor in the enzymic hydroxylation of proline to hydroxyproline. Hydroxyproline is a chemical found in collagen and other related fibrous proteins. Collagen and these other proteins act as the connective tissue fibers that hold cells together, the intercellular cement substance between cells, and the matrix of bone. Vitamin C also functions as an antioxidant, and plays a role in the transfer of plasma iron and its incorporation into tissue ferritin, a storage form of iron. Vitamin C is also involved in other hydroxylation reactions, but its importance in these reactions is unclear. It also plays a role in maintaining normal oxidation of the essential amino acid, tyrosine. Vita-min C aids in the absorption of calcium and iron, and is involved in the synthesis of hormones, including thyroid hormone. Deficiency in this vitamin causes a loss of integrity of many tissues of the body because of the lack of cement substances and collagen fibers and may also decrease resistance to infection.

Vitamin C is synthesized in the liver of some birds during the conversion of glucose; therefore, its addition to the diet is not seen as mandatory by some experts. However, some fruit-eating birds, many passerines, and some others do require an exogenous source. It is my personal opinion that the importance of this vitamin is underestimated in psittacine birds, particularly during times of increased need, such as reproduction, growth, illness, and stress. Vitamin C is highly soluble in water, and much is lost in the cooking of foods by leaching out of the vitamin in the water. It is easily destroyed by transport, storage, processing, light, air, and heat; therefore, fresh, unprocessed foods are considered the best sources.

Choline: Choline's description as a vitamin is of some question, but its importance as a metabolite in the body is undeniable. Choline is essential as a precursor of acetylcholine, is found in phospholipids, and is a source of methyl groups to quaternary nitrogen and sulfonium compounds. Acetylcholine is the chemical substance

Fruits are high in vitamin C.

that transmits nerve impulses from one cell to another. Phospholipids are major components of cell membranes. The phospholipid lecithin is required for the metabolism of fat and the prevention of the abnormal accumulation of fat in the liver. It does this by oxidizing and transporting fatty acids from the liver. Quaternary nitrogen and sulfonium compounds refer to different types of protein that are of a particular type of configuration. Hemoglobin is an example of one of these compounds.

Choline is synthesized in adequate amounts in the animal body when sufficient precursors are present, however, these precursors are often deficient in pet birds. Precursors include ethanolamine (from the amino acid serine), and methyl groups from compounds such as methionine (an essential amino acid). It is my opinion that the importance of choline and methionine in the prevention of fatty liver disease is underestimated, and that it is impor-

tant to ensure that these two elements are included in the diet on a regular basis. Choline deficiency is also known to cause feather depigmentation in baby cockatiels.

Minerals in Detail

The Macrominerals

Calcium: Calcium is the chief mineral constituent of the body, and is required in the diet in larger amounts than any other mineral. Calcium performs four key functions in the body. First, in conjunction with phosphorus, it forms an integral part of bone mineralization in the form of calcium-phosphorus salts. Second, it is an integral part of cell membranes, where it functions in maintaining cell membrane integrity and normal permeability. Third, it forms the link between excitation and contraction in all forms of muscle, and plays a similar role in the excitation and secretion of the glands of the body. Fourth, it acts throughout the body as a regulator, activator, or inhibitor of key enzymes, such as blood clotting. Thus, virtually all key processes in the body are dependent on the availability of calcium.

Calcium deficiency results in a myriad of health problems related to its various functions within the body. Contrary to popular opinion that bone, once formed, doesn't change, bone is a very dynamic organ. It continually undergoes remodeling throughout life. Calcium and phosphorus are essential to this process. If insufficient amounts of calcium are absorbed from the intestine, the mineralization process of bone cannot keep pace with the synthesis of organic bone matrix. When this occurs, signs of rickets or osteomalacia appear.

Most, (about 99 percent), of the calcium found in the body is in the bones, however, a small, but extremely important, portion of calcium is found in the blood plasma and interstitial fluid. Because it is such an important mineral, its concentration in the blood plasma is very closely regulated by a number of substances. The role of vitamin D has already been discussed. Phosphorus is also very important, and will be discussed in detail later. What is important to mention here is that the proper ratio of calcium to phosphorus must exist in order for these minerals to function optimally. Parathyroid hormone, produced by the parathyroid gland, and calcitonin, secreted by the thyroid gland, also play an essential role.

The maintenance of serum calcium levels is at the expense of bone; in other words, the body would rather weaken the skeleton than give up the calcium needed for all its other functions. When the body needs to withdraw calcium from the bone, the process is called demineralization. Too much demineralization (losses of one-third or higher amounts of calcium) results in spontaneous fractures, soft bones, and locomotor disturbances. Paralysis, weakness, and central nervous system disturbances in the form of seizures, are signs of deficiency related to its role in nerve impulse transmission.

When a diet is deficient or improperly balanced in calcium, phosphorus, or vitamin D_3, the parathyroid gland will evoke a rapid response aimed at maintaining a normal plasma calcium level. If calcium deficiency is long-term, the parathyroid gland will undergo a process called hyperplasia (excess growth) as a compensatory mechanism for maintaining plasma calcium levels. This condition is called secondary nutritional hyperparathyroidism, which simply means excess parathyroid growth secondary to dietary causes.

Eggshell is almost entirely formed of calcium, in the form of calcium carbonate. The calcium required for eggshell production is derived from intestinal absorption and/or bone resorption. The medullary (inner) bone is the most important source of calcium for eggshell formation, but when these reserves are gone, the cortical (outer) bone will also be used.

Calcium deficiency is an extremely common problem in pet birds. Not only are seeds themselves notoriously deficient in calcium, but also the fatty acids present in the oils of seeds such as sunflower and safflower seeds combine with calcium to form insoluble soaps, even further decreasing its absorption. Phytic acid, a substance found in whole grains, also binds with calcium and other minerals and prevents their absorption. Muscle meats are also low in calcium, but are high in phosphorus, causing an imbalance in the calcium:phosphorus ratio as well as a deficiency of calcium itself. Oxalic acid, present in some vegetables, combines with calcium and prevents its absorption. Because of this, some nutritionists have advised that feeding some foods, such as broccoli or spinach, may be harmful. It is important to note, however, that spinach, broccoli, kale, and chard are extremely good sources of calcium themselves, and that only a small amount of calcium is bound up by the oxalic acid. Rhubarb leaves, however, do concentrate oxalic acid and should not be fed.

In poultry, a calcium:phosphorus ratio of 3:2 is considered optimum. Therefore, the diet for egg-laying chickens generally contains 1 percent calcium and 0.7 percent phosphorus, depending on the energy level of the diet. In psittacine nutrition, however, the optimum value has not yet been determined, and there is some variation in the ratios recommended by various avian practitioners and food manufacturers. It may be found that the requirement for calcium during egg production may indeed be 1 percent, especially as we breed these birds more intensively and increase our egg yields. Nonetheless, it should be noted that these high levels of calcium are required for egg production, and not for maintenance; one of the reasons why breeding rations should not be fed year-round, even to breeding birds.

Phosphorus: As you have probably already noticed in the discussion of the elements of nutrition so far, the mineral phosphorus is mentioned time and time again. Phosphorus, and organic phosphorus compounds, are part of the structure of all body cells, and are intimately involved in many key physiological and biochemical reactions. First, in conjunction with calcium, phosphorus forms an integral part of bone mineralization in the form of calcium-phosphorus salts. Second, phosphorus is an integral part of cell membranes, in the form of phospholipids. Phospholipids are active determinants of cell permeability. Third, it is an integral part of both DNA and RNA, the genetic compounds responsible for cell reproduction, growth, and protein synthesis. Fourth, it also plays a role in acid-base metabolism as part of the buffering capacity of body tissues and fluids. Fifth, it is an important part of many enzyme systems, including alkaline phosphatase. Sixth, it is a constituent of the high-energy compound called ATP, which is involved in all energy reactions essential for cellular activity. Because all biological events are dependent on energy, it is easy to see how indispensable phosphorus is. Thus, as with calcium, phosphorus plays a role in virtually all key processes within the body.

Sixty to 80 percent of the total phosphorus of cereal grains and oil seeds exists as phytic acid. Phytic acid is organically bound, and is largely unavailable to birds for utilization. An excess of iron, aluminum, or magnesium interferes with phosphorus absorption through the formation of insoluble phosphate compounds.

Phosphorus deficiency rarely occurs in pet birds. In fact, despite the importance of phosphorus to the body, excess phosphorus intake is a common problem. As mentioned in the discussion of calcium, phosphorus levels in the blood are inversely proportional; even if the phosphorus level consumed is within normal limits, if the intake of calcium is low, the level of phosphorus in the bloodstream may be too high, and the body will draw calcium from the bones in order to compensate. Birds on a seed-only diet invariably consume too high a level of phosphorus in relation to their calcium intake.

Foods with a good calcium: phosphorous ratio include watercress, broccoli, dandelion greens, leeks, carrots, swiss chard, spinach, green beans, and cheese. Foods high in phosphorous include grapes,

Seeds are deficient in many essential nutrients.

lettuce, pears, cauliflower, tomatoes, apples, mealworms, corn, almonds, sunflower seeds, and peanuts.

Magnesium: As with calcium and phosphorus, magnesium is involved in many biological functions. Seventy percent of magnesium in the body is found in bone, although its concentration in soft tissue is greater than any other mineral except potassium. Cardiac muscle, nervous tissue, and skeletal muscle all depend on a proper balance between calcium and magnesium ions. Magnesium is an active component of several enzyme systems. It plays a role in protein synthesis, muscle relaxation, carbohydrate metabolism, and energy release, and is also involved in calcium and phosphorus metabolism. Magnesium is also an important constituent of eggshell.

Magnesium deficiency is unusual, but it may occur after prolonged vomiting or diarrhea, in protein deficiency, or when excess calcium increases the excretion of magnesium through the urine.

Sodium: Sodium is the major cation (positively-charged particle) of the extracellular fluid, involved in acid-base equilibrium that regulates the pH of blood. Its most important role is in regulating water balance and body fluid volume by maintaining the osmotic balance of body fluids and tissues. Nerve transmission and muscle contraction involve temporary exchange of extracellular sodium and intracellular potassium across cell membranes. It is also involved in the absorptive processes of monosaccharides, amino acids, pyrimidines, and bile salts. Sodium is also needed in egg production. All these functions depend upon the active transport of sodium across cell membranes. This transport mechanism is referred to as the "sodium pump." Sodium metabolism is regulated primarily by aldosterone, a hormone of the adrenal cortex that promotes reabsorption of sodium from the kidney tubules.

Sodium is deficient in most seed diets. Sodium is also lost through the kidney in the form of sodium chloride or sodium phosphate. Major losses of sodium lead to a lowering of osmotic pressure, and from there to water loss and dehydration. Compensating for this loss requires replenishment of water and sodium.

Chlorine: Chlorine combines with metals, nonmetals, and organic materials to form hundreds of different compounds. Sodium chloride is the source used most often by the body. Chlorine is the major anion (negatively-charged particle) of extracellular fluid. As part of sodium chloride, it plays a role in water balance, acid base balance, and osmotic pressure. It transfers readily between body fluids and red blood cells as a homeostatic mechanism for the control of blood pH. It is also necessary for the formation of hydrochloric acid, the acid present in the stomach used for digestion of food. It also functions as an activator for amylase, a digestive enzyme produced primarily by the pancreas.

Chlorine deficiency can lead to alkalosis because of a decrease of hydrogen ions in the extracellular fluid. Alkalosis refers to a condition in which the pH of the blood becomes too basic, or alkaline. When this occurs, a severe overexcitability of the nervous system results in excessive initiation of signals in many areas of the brain and peripheral nerves.

Excessive loss of chloride ions can occur through excess loss of gastric secretions during vomiting, or by deficiencies in the diet. The optimum ratio between sodium and chloride is approximately 1:1; excess sodium can lead to alkalosis, and excess chloride can lead to acidosis.

Potassium: Potassium is the chief cation of the intracellular fluid.

It contributes to the pH and osmolarity of the fluid inside the cells in much the same way sodium does to the extracellular fluid. Nerve and muscle cells are rich in potassium. Potassium is involved in the transmission of nerve impulses by developing a membrane potential much the same way as sodium does. It influences the contractibility of smooth, skeletal, and cardiac muscle, and has an effect on muscle irritability. Potassium is also involved in glycogen formation, glucose degradation, and protein metabolism. Potassium deficiency leads to an impairment of nerve impulse transmission. This can result in impaired neuromuscular functioning and damage of skeletal, smooth, and cardiac muscle.

Dietary deficiency of potassium is unlikely, but excessive water loss or uncontrolled diabetes may cause potassium depletion. The potassium requirement of chickens is 0.2 to 0.25 percent of the diet; turkeys, by contrast, require a level of 0.4 to 0.5 percent. This requirement is affected somewhat by the growth rate of the animal and the protein level in the diet.

Sulfur: Most of the sulfur in the body is contained in the essential amino acids, cystine and methionine. Proteins vary in their sulfur content depending on their composition of amino acids, but most proteins contain approximately 1 percent sulfur. Sulfur is also contained in saliva, red blood cells,

Bananas are rich in potassium.

the chemical glutathione (present in all cells), and in chondroitin sulfate. Chondroitin sulfate is involved in the structural nature of skin, feathers, keratin, cartilage, bone, tendons, and blood vessel walls. Sulfur is also involved in the storage and release of energy, is part of the genetic material of cells, is in the vitamins biotin and thiamine, is a promoter of several enzyme reactions, and is involved in blood clotting. It also combines with certain toxic materials that enter the body so they can be passed out in the urine.

Because, for metabolic purposes, sulfur is necessary as the preformed amino acids, sulfur deficiencies are reflected as deficiencies in the sulfur-containing amino acids. When sulfur-containing protein intake is adequate, sulfur intake is adequate as well, because the sulfur-containing amino acids can supply all the sulfur needed by the body.

The Microminerals

Manganese: Manganese is considered a micromineral, in that only very small amounts of it are required in the diet for it to perform its various functions. However, it plays such an essential role in the body that a deficiency does produce a number of readily apparent clinical signs. Manganese is involved in mucopolysaccharide and glycoprotein synthesis. Mucopolysaccharides are involved in cartilage, tendon, and bone structure. Manganese, along with vitamin K, is involved in prothrombin synthesis, which is part of the clotting mechanism. Manganese is also a cofactor in many biotin-requiring carboxylase reactions.

Corn is extremely low in manganese, as are animal by-products. Because of the relatively high levels of manganese required by poultry and the low levels present in most poultry diet ingredients, manganese supplementation in the diet is essential. It is suspected that this is also true for psittacines, thus the addition of manganese to pelleted rations for psittacine birds.

Iron: Iron functions in the body through its oxidation-reduction activity and its ability to transport electrons. Iron can be utilized from both organic and inorganic sources in the diet. Iron in foods occurs primarily in the ferric form in combination with other organic compounds. Therefore, it must be released from the organic compound and reduced before it can be absorbed. Iron compounds are ionized by hydrochloric acid in the stomach and reduced to the ferrous state in the duodenum of the small intestine, where they are absorbed. Iron absorption is controlled by the body's requirements, thus it is believed that an active carrier system must be involved in transporting iron across the intestinal mucosal cell membrane. Once in the body, iron can be used in a number of ways. It can form the heme compounds, hemoglobin and myoglobin; the heme enzymes, mitochondrial and microsomal cytochromes, catalase, and peroxidase; or the non-heme compounds, flavin-iron enzymes, transferrin, and ferritin. Mitochondrial and microsomal heme enzymes are involved in energy metabolism. Transferrin is involved in iron transport, and ferritin is a form of iron storage. Ferritin may be incorporated into protoporphyrin to form heme, or into the prosthetic groups of various enzymes as an iron-porphyrin complex. Thus, iron plays an essential role in the oxygen-carrying capacity of blood and in various enzyme systems involved in energy metabolism.

Iron deficiency in birds is common. Iron is released from transferrin in the subcutaneous capillary bed, where it combines with the proteins of the dermis, and is carried slowly to the surface of the skin where it is lost as the skin cells flake off. Increased iron can be lost through blood loss. Dietary factors may interfere with iron absorption. High levels of phosphates reduce absorption, as does phytic acid. Only 10 percent of iron in food is absorbed. Adrenal cortical hormones play a part in regulating the level of iron in plasma; during stress, when the hypothalamus, adenohypophysis, and adrenal cortex are activated, plasma iron levels decrease.

Reducing substances in the diet, such as vitamin C or cysteine, may aid in the reduction of iron from the ferric state to the ferrous state and thus aid in its absorption.

Zinc: Zinc is essential in the normal functioning of the body. Zinc plays a part in over seventy different enzyme systems involved in the metabolism of carbohydrates, fats, nucleic acids, and proteins, including alcohol dehydrogenase, carbonic anhydrase, alkaline phophatase, and the DNA and RNA polymerases. It is also part of the hormone insulin and plays an important role in the transport of vitamin A from its storage in the liver so that it can be used by the body. Most of the zinc within the body is found in bones, with much of the remainder found in the skin, feathers, and keratin of the beak and nails.

Infections, injuries, or other physical causes of stress can cause zinc to be lost in the urine. Whole grains contain phytic acid, a substance that combines with zinc and prevents its absorption. Zinc absorption is also reduced by the presence of iron.

Copper: Copper is present in all body tissues, with the highest concentrations present in liver, heart, brain, and kidney. It plays an essential role in a number of important enzyme systems. A few of these include cytochrome A, cytochrome oxidase, tyrosinase, superoxide dismutase, ascorbic acid oxidase, plasma monoamine oxidase, ferroxidase, and ceruloplasmin. Cytochrome A and cytochrome oxidase are respiratory pigments involved in electron transfer as it relates to iron, hemoglobin, oxygen utilization, and thus to energy metabolism. Tyrosinase converts tyrosine to melanin, the pigment of skin and feathers. Superoxide dismutase is important in trapping free radicals, the chemicals present in the body that can do damage to cells and enzyme systems. Ascorbic acid oxidase is involved in vitamin C metabolism. Plasma monoamine oxidase is involved in the metabolism of epinephrine, the chemical of "fight or flight" response. Ferroxidase converts iron to the proper valence (electrical charge) for transport by the glycoprotein transferrin. Ceruloplasmin functions in transporting copper in blood. Copper is also essential in cross-linking the amino acid lysine in elastin. Elastin is the basic structural element of elastic connective tissue. It is also believed that copper is required in the oxidation of sulfur in keratin synthesis.

Copper is absorbed mainly in the upper part of the small intestine. The availability of copper is influenced by its chemical form; the sulfides are less available than the carbonates, oxides, or sulfates. In general, only 5 to 10 percent of ingested copper is absorbed and retained; the rest is excreted in the feces. Bile is the major pathway of excretion of absorbed copper. Iron, zinc, molybdenum, and sulfate can all have an effect on the absorption and excretion of copper. The minimum requirement of copper in the diet of chickens is 4 to 6 ppm.

Cobalt: Cobalt is widely distributed in nature, though usually just in trace amounts. Cobalt is essential for the production of vitamin B_{12} by the microorganisms of the intestine. The clinical signs of cobalt deficiency would be the same as those seen in vitamin B_{12} deficiency.

Cobalt deficiency in birds is a direct result of vitamin B_{12} deficiency, because the cobalt needed by the body is provided by ingesting substances rich in vitamin B_{12}. The estimated dietary requirement of vitamin B_{12} for chicks is 0.01 to 0.02 ppm (10 to 20 micrograms per kilogram of diet), which would equal 0.0005 to 0.001 ppm of cobalt.

Iodine: Iodine is essential in the synthesis of thyroid hormone. It is readily absorbed by the digestive tract, and is then oxidized in the thyroid gland and bound to the tyrosine molecules of thyroglobulin, a glycoprotein. Hydrolysis of thyroglobulin yields thyroxine. The chief function of thyroxine is to control cellular energy transductions. Deficiency of iodine results in decreased synthesis and secretion of functional thyroid hormone, and enlargement of the thyroid develops. Hypothyroidism and goiter refer to two diseases related to iodine metabolism.

The amount of iodine present in vegetables and grains depends on the species of plant, the amount of iodine that was present in the soil in which they were grown, the climate, and the type of fertilizer used. Iodine-deficient areas are found in the interior of all countries, especially where wind or rainfall are unable to carry traces of iodine from the sea. Certain plants have goitrogenic activity; that is they have a direct effect on the functioning of the thyroid gland. There are several different types of goitrogenic substances in plants: thiocyanates, perchlorates, thioglycosides, and thiouracils. Thiocyanates and perchlorates act by inhibiting the selective concentration of iodine by the thyroid gland. Their actions are reversible with the addition of iodine to the diet. Thioglycosides and thiouracil act by inhibiting hormonogenesis in the thyroid gland. Their actions are not reversible, or are only partially so with iodine supplementation. Vegetables with goitrogenic activity include cabbage, brussels sprouts, rutabagas, cauliflower, turnips, and peanuts. Because heat destroys goitrogens, these substances are generally considered harmful only if large quantities are eaten raw.

Selenium: Selenium is found in all body tissues, but is in highest concentration in the liver, kidney, spleen, pancreas, and testicles. Its activity appears to be closely related to the antioxidative functions of vitamin E, in that it will protect the body from certain signs of vitamin E deficiency, such as exudative diathesis in chickens. It will not, however, protect against certain other signs of vitamin E deficiency, such as muscular dystrophy, encephalomalacia, or reproductive failure. Selenium is a component of the enzyme glutathione peroxidase, and protects cells from damage by destroying hydrogen peroxide, a by-product of cell metabolism. It also enhances the overall activity of the alpha-ketoglutarate oxidase system, the enzyme system important in energy metabolism.

The amount of selenium present in grains depends on the amount present in the soil where they are grown; certain areas of the country are selenium deficient, whereas in other areas excess selenium is present and can result in toxicity.

Fluoride: Fluoride is found in bones and body fluid. If fluoride is available during the development of bones, it is incorporated into their structure. This is accomplished by the replacement of a hydroxyl group by fluorine in the formation of apatite, the small, hexonal crystals of inorganic material in bone. Apparently this substitution increases the crystal size and perfection of the crystal structure. Clinical signs of deficiency are rarely apparent, but bones formed without fluoride are more susceptible to osteoporosis.

Fluoride is widely but unevenly distributed in nature. In most municipal water supplies fluoride has been added to the drinking water at levels of 1 ppm, and birds can utilize the fluoride present from this source. Depending on the area of the country, however, well water may not provide fluoride. Intestinal absorption of fluoride is variable, and is likely due to the varying solubility of that ingested; fluorine in natural feedstuffs or in rock phosphate seems better tolerated than sodium fluoride, which is highly soluble. Poultry seem to have a higher tolerance to fluoride, possibly due to lower absorption and higher excretion of the element.

Chromium: Chromium is a micromineral that is not yet well researched. It is part of the glucose tolerance factor, a substance that regulates the metabolism of glucose in the body by increasing the action of insulin. When chromium is lacking, insulin doesn't function properly. It may also play a role in the configuration of the RNA molecule, and in certain enzyme systems involved in carbohydrate and fat metabolism.

Molybdenum: Molybdenum is found in bone, skin, muscle, and liver. It acts as a cofactor in several enzyme systems, including aldehyde oxidase, nitrate reductase, and xanthine oxidase. Aldehyde oxidase is involved in carbohydrate metabolism. Nitrate reductase is an important enzyme in the formation of ammonia, which can then be used by the body to form amino groups, the building blocks of amino acids and, thus, proteins. Xanthine oxidase catalyzes the oxidation of purines and reduced pyridine nucleotides, and is thus involved in the formation of uric acid, the waste product of protein metabolism in birds. For this reason, it is believed that birds may have a higher requirement for molybdenum than some other species, because other species degrade only a few compounds to uric acid and likely do not require as much of the xanthine oxidase enzyme. No characteristic syndrome of molybdenum deficiency has been recognized, but it may have an influence on growth rate.

Sulfates may interfere with the absorption and excretion of molybdenum.

Silicon: Silicon is found in abundance in nature, exceeding by far every other element except oxygen. It has been found to be essential for normal growth and development in chicks, probably because of its presence in some of the acid mucopolysaccharides. Acid mucopolysaccharides include the chemicals hyaluronic acid, chondroitin, and heparin that are present in synovial fluid, the cornea, and blood, respectively.

Because silicon is so widely available in the diet, clinical signs of silicon deficiency are unknown. However, it has been found that the silicon content of tissues decreases with age, and this finding has been implicated in the development of atherosclerosis.

Other Trace Elements: Several other trace elements have been found in animal tissues, but their importance to physiological well-being is not yet known. Bromine, vanadium, nickel, arsenic, tin, rubidium, aluminum, and titanium are included in this list, and others may yet be found. Bromine has been reported to increase the growth rate of chicks. Vanadium has been suggested as having a role in promoting growth, altering lipid metabolism, and lowering cholesterol. Nickel appears essential in chicks for the development of normal skin, cell membranes, lipid metabolism, growth, and DNA metabolism. Arsenic may control harmful intestinal organisms. Tin may have a role as an oxidation-reduction reaction catalyst.

Food sources for these microminerals are not generally described, and they appear to be required in such minute amounts that a well-rounded diet with some animal protein source should provide sufficient levels. Nonetheless, the significance of these trace elements may become more apparent as research continues.

The Essential Amino Acids

Amino acids serve as the building blocks of protein in the body. They are also involved in a myriad of other functions, by acting as precursors of many other biomolecules, such as hormones, purines, pyrimidines, porphyrins, and some vitamins. They can also serve as a source of energy, particularly when consumed in excess of their need for other functions. When used for energy, their amino groups are lost and their remaining carbon skeletons undergo one of two processes; gluconeogenesis, whereby they are converted to the sugar glucose that can be stored for later use; or oxidation to carbon dioxide via the tricarboxylic acid cycle with a concomitant release of energy. Protein metabolism is a dynamic process; it is estimated that a 155-pound (70-kg) man on an average diet turns over 14 ounces (400 g) of protein per day. One quarter of this is converted to glucose or undergoes oxidative degradation and is replaced daily from the diet; the remaining three quarters are recycled.

Some of the 20 amino acids can be manufactured within the body from chemical precursors. Those amino acids that must be supplied in the diet are known as the essential amino acids. Leucine, isoleucine, lysine, methionine, phenylalanine, threonine, tryptophan, and valine are considered essential. Arginine and histidine were formerly considered essential, but can be synthesized in sufficient quantity to meet metabolic needs, though addition to the diet is still warranted. Glutamic acid, glycine, and proline are often added to this list because they are needed for optimal growth in chickens and therefore may also be important in pet birds.

It is my opinion that many essential amino acid deficiencies go unrecognized, and likely play a role in many poorly defined ailments, illnesses, growth disturbances, and reproductive failures. Some of the roles of the essential amino acids,

Methionine deficiency can cause fatty liver disease, resulting in beak overgrowth.

and signs of their deficiency that have been recognized, are described in Table 4, page 49. It is important to note that this is not a definitive list; it is simply a few examples of the many roles these amino acids play.

Most seeds are low in lysine, tryptophan, and arginine. Soybeans, corn, cottonseed, safflower seeds, and peanuts are low in lysine and methionine.

Conclusion

From this detailed discussion of vitamins, minerals, and amino acids, one can begin to appreciate the complexities of nutrition. In particular, one can better appreciate how interactive all the elements of nutrition are. Personally, I have a great respect for those people who have devoted their lives to the study of nutrition. It is no wonder that so many questions remain unanswered; each time a certain chemical or enzymic pathway is discovered, new interactions are found, resulting in a reevaluation of what was known until that time.

Still, it is important not to become bewildered by all this information. A balanced diet can be achieved, if you keep one golden rule in mind: All things in moderation. The next section of the book deals with nutrition and the pet bird. This section will provide a simple, step-by-step approach to nutrition for your pet bird.

TABLE 1
Dietary Sources of Vitamins and Minerals

Vitamin A

Food Source	Quantity	Amount (IU)
Beef liver, fried	1/3 ounce	5,000
Dandelion leaves, raw	1/5 cup	5,000
Sweet potatoes, boiled	1/2 medium	5,000
Apricots, dried	1/3 cup	5,000
Spinach, cooked	1/3 cup	5,000
Carrot, raw	1 whole	5,000
Red chili peppers, dried	1/2 tablespoon	5,000
Broccoli, cooked	1 medium stalk	4,000
Squash, cooked	1/4 cup	2,150
Cantaloupe	1/4 medium	1,500

Vitamin D

Food Source	Quantity	Amount (IU)
Product 19, Kellogg's	1/4 cup	50
Most, Kellogg's	1/4 cup	50
Egg, cooked	1 medium	27
Prime vitamins	1 milliliter	26.4
Beef liver, cooked	1/3 ounce	9

Vitamin E

Food Source	Quantity	Amount (IU)
Wheat germ oil	1 teaspoon	9.4
Most, Kellogg's	1/4 cup	7.5
Sweet potato	1/2 medium	4.9
Sunflower seed, hulled	1 tablespoon	1.75
Walnuts, shelled	4 halves	1.7
Almonds, shelled	2 whole	1
Wheat germ	1 tablespoon	1
Brussels sprouts	1 large	0.76
Asparagus	1 spear	0.74
Egg, cooked	1 large	0.6

Vitamin K

Food Source	Quantity	Amount (micrograms)
Turnip greens, cooked	1/3 cup	325
Cabbage, cooked	1/3 cup	62.5

Broccoli, cooked	1/4 cup	40
Spinach, cooked	1/4 cup	40
Asparagus, cooked	1/3 cup	28.5
Cheese	1 ounce	14
Beef liver, cooked	1/3 ounce	12
Egg, cooked	1 medium	11
Green peas, cooked	1/3 cup	9.5
Green beans, cooked	1/4 cup	5

Vitamin B₁ (Thiamine)

Food Source	Quantity	Amount (milligrams)
Product 19, Kellogg's	1 ounce	1.5
Lentils, cooked, drained	1/4 cup	0.9
Sunflower seeds, hulled	1/4 cup	0.87
Red kidney beans, cooked	1/4 cup	0.75
Brazil nuts, shelled	1/4 cup	0.37
Sesame seeds	1/4 cup	0.28
Pecan halves	1/4 cup	0.24
Peanuts, shelled	1/4 cup	0.12
Green peas, boiled	1/4 cup	0.11
Almonds, shelled	1/4 cup	0.08

Vitamin B₂ (Riboflavin)

Food Source	Quantity	Amount (milligrams)
Beef liver	1/3 ounce	0.4
Broccoli, steamed	1 spear	0.37
Brewer's yeast	1 tablespoon	0.34
Almonds, shelled	1/4 cup	0.29
Cottage cheese, 2% BF	1/4 cup	0.11
Cheddar cheese	1 ounce	0.11
Spinach, cooked	1/4 cup	0.11
Yogurt	1 ounce	0.06

Niacin

Food Source	Quantity	Amount (milligrams)
Tuna, canned in water	1/4 cup	8.5
Peanuts, shelled	1/4 cup	7.8
Chicken, cooked	1/8 breast	5
Sesame seeds	1/4 cup	5
Sunflower seeds, hulled	1/4 cup	3.9
Brewer's yeast	1 tablespoon	3.6

Ground beef, cooked	1/4 patty	2.5
Salmon, canned	1 ounce	2
Eggs, cooked	1 large	1.6

Vitamin B₆ (Pyridoxine)

Food Source	Quantity	Amount (milligrams)
Egg yolk, cooked	1 yolk	0.3
Beef liver, cooked	1 ounce	0.28
Tuna, canned	1 ounce	0.26
Chicken, cooked	1 ounce	0.20
Corn Flakes, Kellogg's	1/4 cup	0.17
Banana	1/4 medium	0.15
Corn, canned	1/4 cup	0.15
Sunflower seeds, hulled	1 tablespoon	0.11
Brussels sprouts, cooked	1 large	0.1
Squash, cooked	1/4 cup	0.1

Pantothenic Acid

Food Source	Quantity	Amount (milligrams)
Beef liver, cooked	1 ounce	2.18
Beef kidney, cooked	1 ounce	1.1
Egg, cooked	1 large	0.8
Grapefruit	1/4 medium	0.3
Cauliflower, raw	1/4 cup	0.28
Cheddar cheese	1 ounce	0.14
Corn, canned	1/4 cup	0.14
Banana	1/4 medium	0.1

Folic Acid

Food Source	Quantity	Amount (milligrams)
Brewer's yeast	1 tablespoon	310
Chicken liver, cooked	1 medium	154
Broccoli, raw	1 spear	107
Product 19, Kellogg's	1/4 cup	100
Lentils, cooked	1/4 cup	95
Chick peas, cooked	1/4 cup	75
Orange	1 medium	60
Peanuts, shelled	1/4 cup	40
Brussels sprouts	1 large	33

Vitamin B$_{12}$

Food Source	Quantity	Amount (micrograms)
Beef liver, cooked	1 ounce	23
Clams, canned	1/4 cup	10
Chicken liver, cooked	1 ounce	6.9
Salmon, canned	1 ounce	2
Tuna, canned	1 ounce	0.85
Beef, cooked	1 ounce	0.73
Egg, cooked	1 medium	0.6
Cheddar cheese	1 ounce	0.3

Biotin

Food Source	Quantity	Amount (micrograms)
Beef liver, cooked	1 ounce	28.6
Cauliflower	1/4 cup	4.25
Banana	1 medium	4
Grapefruit	1/4 medium	1.5
Cheddar cheese	1 ounce	1

Vitamin C

Food Source	Quantity	Amount (milligrams)
Broccoli, raw	1 spear	141
Orange, peeled	1 medium	70
Kiwi	1 large	68
Cantaloupe	1/4 medium	57
Papaya, peeled	1/2 medium	48
Green pepper, raw	1/2 medium	40
Brussels sprouts, cooked	1/4 cup	25
Tomato, raw	1 small	22
Mango, peeled	1/4 medium	10
Pear, raw	1 medium	7

Choline

Food Source	Quantity	Amount (milligrams)
Egg yolk, cooked	1 medium	255
Beef, cooked	1 ounce	180
Fish, cooked	1 ounce	60

Calcium

Food Source	Quantity	Amount (milligrams)
Cuttlebone	1 gram	400

Swiss cheese	1 ounce	270
Yogurt	1/4 cup	88
Turnip greens, cooked	1/4 cup	63
Salmon, canned	1 ounce	55
Kale, cooked	1/4 cup	40
Tofu	1 ounce	38
Navy beans	1/4 cup	25
Broccoli	1/4 cup	25

Phosphorus (Increase in dietary phosphorus seldom needed)

Food Source	QuantityAmount (milligrams)	
Almonds, shelled	1 ounce	143
Peanuts, shelled	1 ounce	115
Chicken, cooked	1 ounce	77
Lima beans, cooked	1/4 cup	74
Kidney beans, cooked	1/4 cup	70
Tuna, canned in water	1 ounce	66
Potato, baked	1/2 medium	58
Beef, cooked	1 ounce	53
Broccoli, steamed	1/4 cup	40

Magnesium

Food Source	QuantityAmount (milligrams)	
Chick-peas, cooked	1/4 cup	30
Black-eyed peas, cooked	1/4 cup	30
Lima beans, cooked	1/4 cup	25
Broccoli	1/4 cup	24
Fig, dried	1 large	11

Sodium

Food Source	QuantityAmount (milligrams)	
Table salt	1 teaspoon	2,325
Cheddar cheese	1 ounce	168
Corn, canned	1/4 cup	140
Beets, canned	1/4 cup	125
Peanut butter	1 tablespoon	97
Carrots, canned	1/4 cup	93
Egg, cooked	1 large	61
Celery, raw	1/4 cup	28
Carrots, boiled	1/4 cup	27
Beets, boiled	1/4 cup	22

Potassium

Food Source	Quantity	Amount (milligrams)
Potato, baked	1 medium	844
Banana	1 medium	450
Cantaloupe	1/4 medium	400
Lima beans, cooked	1/4 cup	291
Squash, cooked	1/4 cup	267
Orange	1 medium	237
Peanuts, shelled	1 ounce	204
Split peas, cooked	1/4 cup	148
Beef, cooked	1 ounce	116

Iron

Food Source	Quantity	Amount (milligrams)
Pumpkin seeds, dried	1/4 cup	5
Sunflower seeds, hulled	1/4 cup	2.5
Soybeans, cooked	1/4 cup	2.3
Beef liver, cooked	1 ounce	1.8
Lentils, cooked	1/4 cup	1.75
Spinach, cooked	1/4 cup	1.7
Almonds, shelled	1/4 cup	1.35
Lima beans, cooked	1/4 cup	1.1
Swiss chard, cooked	1/4 cup	1

Zinc

Food Source	Quantity	Amount (milligrams)
Oyster, cooked	1 medium	10
Beef, cooked	1 ounce	1.2
Cheddar cheese	1 ounce	0.8
Egg, cooked	1 large	0.7
Split peas, cooked	1/4 cup	0.5
Brown rice, cooked	1/4 cup	0.4
Potato, baked	1 medium	0.4
Peanut butter	1 tablespoon	0.4
Noodles, enriched	1/4 cup	0.3
Soybeans, cooked	1/4 cup	0.3

Selenium

Food Source	Quantity	Amount (micrograms)
Salmon, canned	1 ounce	21
Tuna, canned	1 ounce	20

Beef liver, cooked	1 ounce	16
Egg noodles	1/3 cup	9.5
Granola	1/4 cup	6

Sulfur
Cheese, eggs, fish, grains, nuts, dried peas, beans

Manganese
Whole grains, nuts, dried peas, beans

Copper
Shellfish, liver, beans, peas, nuts

Cobalt
(See vitamin B_{12})

Iodine
Seafood, some mineral blocks, Lugol's iodine

Chromium
Whole grains, meat, cheese, eggs, yeast

Molybdenum
Liver, wheat germ, whole grains, dried peas, beans

Table 2
Effects of Vitamin/Mineral Deficiency

	Infertility	Soft-Shelled Eggs	Reduced Egg Production	Reduced Hatchability	Retarded Growth	Rickets	Perosis	Bone Deformities	Incoordination, Staggering Gait	Convulsions
VITAMINS										
A		X	X	X	X			X		
D		X	X	X	X	X		X	X	
E	X			X				X		X
K										
B$_1$ (Thiamine)					X					X
B$_2$ (Riboflavin)			X	X	X				X	
Niacin					X					
B$_6$			X	X	X					X
Pantothenic Acid			X	X	X					
Folic Acid				X	X					
B$_{12}$				X	X			X		
Biotin				X	X		X	X	X	
C										
Choline			X	X	X					
MINERALS										
Calcium		X	X	X	X	X	X	X	X	X
Phosphorous			X	X	X	X	X	X	X	
Magnesium					X				X	
Sodium			X	X	X					
Chlorine			X	X	X					X
Potassium										X
Sulfur					X					
Manganese			X	X	X		X			X
Iron										
Zinc	X				X			X		
Copper										
Cobalt					X			X		
Iodine	X									
Selenium					X					

Weakness, Paralysis	Skin Lesions	Poor Plumage, Unthrifty	Nasal/Ocular Discharge, Lesions	Anemia	Decreased Immunity	Increased Bleeding	Egg Binding	OTHER PROBLEMS
	X	X	X		X			Night blindness
		X					X	Rachitic rosary, osteomalacia
X					X	X		Muscle degeneration, exudative diathesis
				X		X		
X								Polyneuritis, heart muscle and nerve degeneration, diarrhea
X		X						Clubbed down feathers, curled-toe paralysis
	X	X						Inflammed oral cavity, digestive disturbances
				X				Anorexia, weight loss
	X	X	X					Spinal cord degeneration, liver dysfunction
		X		X				
		X		X				Slowed production of red blood cells, nervous system damage
	X		X					Loss of toes, limb deformities, fatty liver disease
X					X	X		
		X						Slipped tendons, fatty liver disease, anorexia
X		X				X	X	
		X						
		X						
								Pica (abnormal appetite)
X								
X								Heart arrhythmia, altered gastric motility and secretions
		X						Fatty liver disease
X								
				X				Disorders related to oxygen deprivation
	X	X			X			Delayed wound healing, anorexia
				X				
		X		X				Slowed production of red blood cells, nervous system damage
		X		X				Goiter
X								Exocrine pancreatic degeneration, myocarditis

TABLE 3
Signs of Dietary Excess of Vitamins and Minerals

Vitamin A
Weight loss, joint pain, nausea, bone deformities, muscle soreness, dry and flaky skin, diarrhea, rashes, enlarged liver and spleen, stunted growth, and infertility have been reported.

Excess carotene may cause yellowing of the skin on the soles of the feet.

Vitamin D
At first calcification of bone may be accelerated, but in later stages bone resorption is increased, leading to a demineralized and weakened skeleton and hypercalcemia.

Hypercalcemia results in calcium deposition in the kidneys, heart, joints, arteries, and other tissues, causing irreversible damage.

Especially common in juvenile macaws.

Vitamin E
Large doses may be antagonistic to vitamin A instead of its usual antioxidant effect.

Vitamin K
Overdosage of natural vitamin K has not been reported, but overdosage with synthetic water-soluble vitamin K has caused red blood cell breakdown and jaundice in humans. Overdosage of synthetic vitamin K in humans causes brain damage in infants and pregnant women.

Vitamin B_1
Toxicity has not been reported in pet birds.

Vitamin B_2
High doses will cause the urates to be bright yellow; this may be misinterpreted as liver disease if the observer is not aware that high doses of riboflavin have been administered or consumed.

Niacin
In people, large doses of nicotinic acid have been shown to lower blood cholesterol and triglycerine levels; however, these high doses can also cause blood vessel dilation, tingling and flushing of face, neck, and chest, an itchy skin rash, indigestion, peptic ulcers, injury to the liver, and increased blood levels of uric acid and glucose. High doses of niacinamide do not lower blood cholesterol or triglycerides or cause these adverse reactions.

Vitamin B_6
Increases the excretion of oxalate in the urine, a substance known to increase the risk of kidney or bladder stones in some species of animals. Tingling and numbness of the hands and feet and an inability to walk have been reported in humans.

Pantothenic Acid
Toxicity has not been reported in pet birds, but high doses have caused diarrhea in humans.

Folic Acid
May mask a lack of vitamin B_{12}, delaying recognition of this problem with serious consequences.

Vitamin B_{12}
Toxicity has not been reported in pet birds.

Biotin
Toxicity has not been reported in pet birds.

Vitamin C
Normally excreted in the urine; toxicity from natural sources in the diet would be unlikely.

Excess levels of artificial vitamin C supplementation have resulted in a transient diarrhea in some species of animals and in man, and megadoses are suspected to predispose some species to the formation of calcium oxalate kidney stones.

Choline
Toxicity has not been reported in pet birds.

Calcium
Turkey pullets fed high-calcium diets exhibited nephrosis syndrome with kidney failure and resultant visceral urate deposition (gout complex).

Heavy calcium diets without a concurrent increase in manganese and zinc levels will interfere with absorption of these trace elements and lead to perosis, a type of bone disease.

Phosphorus
Common toxicity resulting in an improper calcium:phosphorus ratio, thus resulting in calcium deficiency.

Magnesium
Diarrhea, decreased egg production, thin-shelled eggs, extreme irritability have been reported in chickens.

Sodium
Excessive thirst, muscular weakness, respiratory distress, wet feces, fluid from the beak, and paralysis of the limbs have been reported.

Chlorine
Toxic effects in pet birds are not known (other than in combination with sodium—i.e., salt toxicity).

Potassium
Dilatation of the heart and eventual heart failure may result.

Sulfur
Can affect the absorption and excretion of copper and molybdenum by the body.
Other toxic effects in pet birds are not known.

Manganese

Toxicity is considered rare under normal circumstances; hens were found to be able to tolerate 1,000 ppm without ill effects.

Iron

Nausea, abdominal discomfort, constipation, or diarrhea have been reported in many animal species. In some cases, excess iron intake can be fatal.

(Possible role of dietary iron in hemochromatosis is discussed in the chapter Diet and Disease.)

Zinc

Anorexia, pancreatic damage, destruction and sloughing of the koilin layer of the gizzard. Can interfere with selenium absorption.

Copper

Destruction and sloughing of the koilin layer of the gizzard, gastroenteritis, and liver and kidney damage have been reported.

Cobalt

Toxicity in pet birds has not been reported, but in other animals inhibition by cobalt of certain respiratory enzymes, such as cytochrome oxidase and succinic dehydrogenase, results in a perception by the body of a lack of oxygen, stimulating a chain of events resulting in the creation of more red blood cells (polycythemia, an increase in the number and concentration of circulating red blood cells).

Iodine

Animals appear to be able to tolerate 50 to 100 times their actual requirements of iodine without ill effect, although enlarged thyroid glands have been reported in some bird species fed excess dietary iodine. In some people, a sensitivity to this mineral may cause them to break out in a rash when an excess amount is ingested.

Selenium

Potential for toxicity is high; 0.1 ppm appears to be beneficial; 5 to 8 ppm are toxic.

Acute toxicity causes severe gastroenteritis and shock. Chronic toxicity can result in abnormal feathers, deformed embryos, and decreased hatchability of fertile eggs.

Fluoride

Reduced food consumption, decreased growth, weight loss, and bone deformities have been reported in some animal species.

Molybdenum

Goutlike symptoms have been reported in some animal species.

TABLE 4
Amino Acid Functions and Signs of Deficiency

Amino Acid	Functions	Signs of Deficiency
Leucine	• intermediate formed during degradation is precursor of cholesterol	• curled tongue in chickens
Isoleucine		• curled tongue in chickens
Lysine	• precursor of substance in collagen	• feather depigmentation in chickens, turkeys, and quail
Methionine	• involved in synthesis of choline needed for liver function • needed for normal musculature	• fatty liver disease • long and deformed beaks • notched feathers, stress marks on feathers in raptors
Phenylalanine		• curled tongue in chickens
Tryptophan	• precursor of serotonin and niacin	• nonspecific
Valine	• precursor of leucine • part of pantothenic acid	• nonspecific
Arginine	• feather formation • formation of normal musculature	• incompletely formed feathers • curled tips on wing feathers • may be related to feather picking
Histidine	• present in hemoglobin • derivatives anserine and carnosine abundant in muscle • forms histamine • can form glutamic acid	• nonspecific
Glutamic acid	• can form proline, hydroxyproline	• needed for optimum growth in chickens
Glycine	• can form serine • functions in formation of purines and porphyrins	• needed for normal musculature • thought to result in incompletely formed feathers
Serine	• can form cysteine • involved in formation of lecithin, cephalin, and sphingomyelin	• nonspecific
Proline	• major amino acid of collagen	• structural features of collagen vary with their proline, hydroxy-proline, and glycine content

Chapter 4
Anatomy and Physiology As It Relates to Nutrition

The first section of this book discussed the basics of nutrition, and how these various elements interact in the avian body. Now that we understand the basics of nutrition, we will discuss how to apply this information to our pet birds.

This section covers the most common questions owners have about pet bird nutrition. It is my hope that this section will be of great use to you on a daily basis, and will send you well on the way to improved health for your pet bird.

Birds are intensely visual animals.

The Eye

It may seem unusual to begin a discussion of anatomy as it relates to nutrition by discussing the eye, yet it is essential to realize that birds are intensely visual animals. Of the five senses, sight is the most acute. Hearing is second; touch, taste, and smell are not as keenly developed.

The bird's eye is large in relation to its head. Its eye contains more cone cells than does the human eye, and thus the avian eye has greater visual acuity and has color vision. For this reason, it is very important to take the visual appeal of food into account when formulating a better balanced diet. You may have already noticed that your bird tends to prefer certain food colors over others. Some owners even report that their birds will refuse to eat out of certain colors of dishes.

You can use the bird's natural visual acuity to your advantage.

Anticipation can be heightened by preparing food in front of the bird on a counter in the kitchen, stimulating its digestive juices, so to speak. If your bird has certain color preferences, you can use these to your advantage. For example, if your bird prefers red dishes to other colors, you can reserve its red dish for new foods you wish to introduce. Put its regular food in a cup color it doesn't like, so that your bird may be encouraged to explore the contents of its preferred dish.

The Nose

The olfactory lobes of the brain that control the sense of smell are very small in birds. The olfactory region of the nose itself is far back in the caudal nasal region, so that nostril plugging can interfere with the sense of smell.

Although the sense of smell does not appear to be as keenly developed in pet birds, it is likely that the smell of certain foods may have an impact on food selection. For this reason, certain pellet manufacturers have added fairly strong fruit or peanut odors to their rations in an effort to stimulate the olfactory appeal of their foods. You can do the same; if your bird loves oranges, a drop of orange extract added to rice, for example, may make it more appealing.

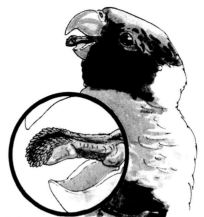

This rainbow lorikeet and all other members of the Loriidae group have a "brush tongue." The word "brush" refers to a cluster of elongated papillae, which increase substantially in length when the tongue is protruded.

The Mouth

Birds also have very few taste buds in comparison to other species; the mallard duck, for example, has only 500 taste buds as opposed to man's 10,000 taste buds. Most of the taste buds are located far back in the mouth region, and not on the tongue in the parrot. Thus, in the parrot, the tongue functions more as a tactile organ than as an organ of taste sensation. In species such as lories and lorikeets, the tongue has been modified; the tip of the tongue possesses a cluster of elongated papillae that are used to help harvest nectar from flowers.

Because the tongue functions more as a tactile organ than as an organ of taste sensation, the texture of food is very important to pet birds. If your bird refuses cooked carrots, it may not be the carrot your bird objects to as much as it is the way it was prepared; try

*The beak
of birds is
variable,
depending
upon their
feeding
habits in
the wild.*

shaving it into curlicues, or offering carrot sticks instead. Some birds have a definite preference for mushy foods, whereas others prefer things that crunch.

The reduced number of taste buds in birds may account for some of their unusual taste preferences. Many parrots enjoy chewing on dried chili peppers, for example. Avi-Sci, Inc., has experimented with different food flavorings and has come up with a product line called Dr. D.'s Spicey Diets. These foods are flavored with hot pepper, marjoram, onion, and paprika—four flavors that the company has found birds seem to prefer. If you find your bird does like onion or peppers, sprinkling a little onion powder or chili powder on an apple wedge or sweet potatoes may be all it takes to have the new food accepted.

The Beak

The beak of pet birds is very variable, depending on their feeding habits in the wild. In parrots, the rhamphotheca, or upper beak, is large and curved, leading to the name hookbill. It is adapted for cracking nuts and for tearing and shredding trees to make nest sites. Finch-like birds, such as canaries, mannikins, and Java sparrows, have short pointed beaks adept at hulling seed and catching insects.

The shape and size of the beak can play an important role in food selection. It has been shown that seed size is a major criterion for seed selection, especially in small birds, such as finches and canaries. If you would like to feed a pelleted ration to your budgerigars, be sure to choose one that has a crumble size that is small enough for easy manipulation in your bird's beak.

The Pharynx

Unlike man, most birds do not possess a soft palate, and there is a direct connection between the pharynx and the oral cavity, which is called the oropharynx. These two regions connect by way of the choana, which is a slit in the roof of the mouth in the hard palate. When the bird eats, this slit closes.

Unlike mammals, which produce a watery saliva, birds' salivary glands produce mostly mucus. In some species the salivary glands also produce amylase, the enzyme that helps to digest starch. The salivary glands of the seed eating species are fairly well developed, and the mucus produced by these glands aids in easing the passage of dry food down the esophagus.

If the production of mucus by these glands is decreased, it is a little more difficult to swallow dry seeds. As discussed in the section on vitamin A, the normal functioning of the salivary glands is partly dependent on adequate levels of vitamin A, in order that the correct cell type is produced within the glands. For those of you with birds on seed-only diets, you may have noticed that your bird often stretches its neck while eating, as though it's having difficulty swallowing. The truth is, if your bird is vitamin A deficient, it may indeed be having trouble swallowing due to a lack of sufficient mucus production by its dysfunctional salivary glands. When the deficiency is corrected, you will observe an improvement in this behavior.

The Esophagus and Crop

The esophagus in birds is very different from that in mammals, and its modification depends on the birds' diet. In all species the esophagus is thin-walled, distensible, and lined with the same kind of cells that line your cheek, and many subepithelial mucous glands that help lubricate the food. In parrot species, the esophagus is dilated in one section to form an outpouching called the crop, or ingluves. The crop is located at the base of the neck just as it enters the thoracic inlet. When the proventriculus and gizzard are full, food can be stored here for a time. Food swells and softens here by the action of water contained in the food, some enzymes in the ingested food material, and in some cases, amylase from the salivary glands, but it is not actually digested in this location. When the proventriculus and gizzard empty, food is moved out of the crop by contractions of the smooth muscle in the esophageal or crop walls.

In some species, such as lories and lorikeets, the crop is relatively small; in others, such as insectivorous birds and owls, the crop may be entirely absent. The crop of pigeons and doves appears to be more active than the crop of parrots, in that mucus, amylase, and serous- and mucous-secreting cells are found in the crop wall. It also produces a "milk" for feeding the young during times of reproduction.

In most species, the food in the crop can undergo reverse peristalsis, so that it can be regurgitated to feed the young, or to feed a partner during the courtship ritual. Some people mistake regurgitation for vomiting. Regurgitation is a willful

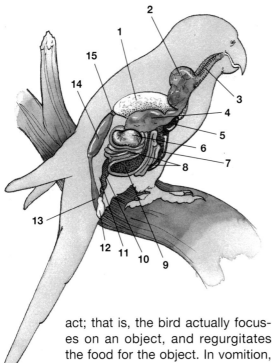

The internal
anatomy
of a parrot:
1. lung.
2. crop.
3. esophagus.
4. proven-
   triculus.
5. heart.
6. gizzard.
7. liver.
8. small
   intestine
9. pancreas
10. large
    intestine.
11. rectum.
12. cloaca.
13. ureter.
14. kidney.
15. adrenal
    gland.

pepsinogen is broken down to pepsin by the hydrochloric acid. Pepsin is the enzyme responsible for breaking down protein to polypeptides, which can then be broken down further by other digestive enzymes.

The gastric juice produced by the proventriculus has a pH of about 0.2 to 0.5, so that it is very acidic, which aids in the digestion of the food. Muscular contractions of the proventriculus push the food into the gizzard.

The Gizzard

The gizzard is also known as the ventriculus. In parrots, the gizzard is a very thick-walled, muscular organ, and this is where the grinding of food takes place, because birds do not possess teeth. It is lined with a hardened, keratinized membrane called the cuticle or koilin, which is produced by excretions of the epithelial lining cells of the gizzard. The asymmetrical contractions of the gizzard, coupled with the rough-ened surface of the koilin and the presence of any grit, is what actually causes the grinding of the food. In birds that don't require much grind-ing of food, such as most species of lories and lorikeets, the gizzard is soft and baglike. The pH of the giz-zard is between 1.5 and 2.5. This acid environment also helps in the digestion of food.

act; that is, the bird actually focus-es on an object, and regurgitates the food for the object. In vomition, the bird is often sitting somewhere, then suddenly flings its head from side to side, throwing mucus and food in all directions, causing the feathers of its head to become pasted with mucus.

After the crop, the esophagus enters the thoracic inlet where it is referred to as the thoracic esopha-gus, and from here it extends down to the proventriculus.

The Proventriculus

The proventriculus is much like the human stomach, in that gastric glands embedded in the wall secrete hydrochloric acid and pepsinogen as well as mucus. The

The Pylorus

The pylorus is the fold that forms a valve that connects the gizzard to the first part of the small intestine, called the duodenum. The pylorus serves to prevent large food particles from entering the duodenum, and normally prevents materials in the duodenum from refluxing back into the gizzard, although in some species (e.g. turkeys) a refluxing of duodenal and upper ileal contents into the gizzard does occur normally several times per hour.

The Small Intestine

The small intestine consists of the duodenum, ileum, and jejunum. The duodenum is shaped in a loop, and the pancreas is located in the center of the loop. The ducts from the pancreas empty into the far end of the duodenum, as do the bile ducts coming from the liver. In birds, the jejunum and ileum are poorly differentiated from one another.

The small intestine is lined with cells that possess small fingerlike projections called microvilli. It is at these microvilli that the actual absorption of food particles takes place. There is a well-defined network of blood capillaries present in the villi, but the villi do not contain lacteals, the small lymphatic ducts that are present in mammalian intestines. Because there are no lacteals present, fats are absorbed directly into the blood and transported from there to the liver. The pH of the intestine ranges from 5.6 to 7.2, depending on the species. Digestion of food in the intestine occurs as a result of the pancreatic enzymes, intestinal secretions and enzymes, and microbial activity. The first quarter of the ileum is the most important site for the absorption of fats, carbohydrates, and ingested proteins. The lower half of the ileum absorbs the breakdown products from body-derived proteins, and the bile acids.

The small intestine also contains circular muscle bands that help move the food along the digestive tract by the action of segmentation and peristalsis.

The length of the small intestine varies with the species; the intestine of parrots is longer than the intestine of mynah birds and lories. The length of the digestive tract influences the rate at which food passes through it; the time required is longest in herbivores like the parrot, and shortest in frugivores (fruit-eating birds) like the lory. The rate of passage can also be influenced by the consistency, water content, and amount of food consumed.

The Pancreas

The pancreas of birds excretes the same chemicals as the mammalian pancreas, namely amylase, lipase, proteinase, and an aqueous solution containing buffering compounds to raise the pH of the intestinal contents to 5.6 to 7.2. It is also the site of secretion of the hormones glucagon, insulin, and somatostatin. The amylases are enzymes that function in carbohydrate metabolism by breaking down starches. Lipase helps split the triglycerides of fat. The proteinases break the polypeptides down into small peptides containing two to six amino acids. From here, enzymes in the mucosal intestinal cells break the peptides down into free amino acids that are transported by the portal blood supply to the liver where they are used in the various processes of protein metabolism. Glucagon is an important hormone in birds, in that it plays a major role in the mobilization of glycerol and fatty acids from fat tissue deposits, and decreases the process of glycogenolysis in the liver, resulting in hyperglycemia, or an increase in blood sugar. Insulin reduces blood sugar levels by causing an increase of metabolism of glucose. Somatostatin is a chemical that acts as an inhibitor of the growth hormone.

The Liver

The liver is an important organ in the process of food digestion and assimilation. It is involved in carbohydrate, fat, and protein metabolism, in blood protein manufacture, in detoxification, in vitamin storage, and in bile formation.

The liver is involved in carbohydrate metabolism in several ways. Glucose and other monosaccharides (simple sugars) are absorbed from the intestine and transported to the liver where they are converted by the liver cells to glycogen, the storage form of glucose. When needed, glycogen is again converted to glucose in the liver. When glycogen reserves have been exhausted, and no new glucose is entering the system from ingested food, the liver can also convert amino acids, fats, glycerol, and other metabolites into glucose. These processes in the liver are controlled by endocrine hormones; glucagon and insulin from the pancreas, epinephrine and corticosterone from the adrenal glands, and thyroxine from the thyroid gland.

The liver is also important in fat metabolism. The liver is the major site of production of both fatty acids and triglycerides (three fatty acids joined to a glycerol molecule). Part of this process involves the manipulation of carbohydrates in the liver to produce the coenzymes and substrates that are required for fat synthesis. Synthesis of phospholipids also takes place in the liver, and is dependent on the presence of choline and methionine.

The liver is the site of production of several important proteins, such as plasma cholinesterase, albumin, prothrombin, fibrinogen, and most of the globulins. Thrombocytes (platelets) are also produced in the liver. The liver also acts as a storage reservoir for vitamin A, vitamin D, iron, and some of the B vitamins.

The liver can detoxify many poisons in the body. Part of the detoxification mechanisms are involved in the formation of the bile pigments bilirubin and biliverdin, a part of bile. Bile also consists of bile salts (the conjugates of bile acids), protein, cholesterol, and inorganic salts. Bile serves three functions: it neutralizes the hydrochloric acid from the proventriculus helping to raise the pH of the intestinal contents; it aids in the digestion of carbohydrates by the action of amylase; and it also plays an important role in emulsifying fats by way of the bile salts. The bile salts are resorbed in the lower ileum and recirculated to the liver to be used again. The green color of bile is caused by the pigment biliverdin, the waste product of hemoglobin metabolism. It is this substance that gives the feces its characteristic green color.

Most parrots do not possess a gallbladder, though many species of birds do. If a gallbladder is present, it acts as a storage site of bile, allowing the bile to become more concentrated as water is resorbed.

The Large Intestine

In some birds, the large intestine consists of paired caeca and a short rectum. Parrots do not possess caeca, but chickens do. As mentioned in our discussion on fiber, the large intestine is very short in birds. For this reason, it is not believed to be as influenced by the effects of fiber as our own digestive tract is. The large intestine serves as the area for water resorption. From the rectum, feces are moved to the cloaca.

The Cloaca

The rectum empties into an area called the cloaca. This is where the kidneys also empty by way of the ureters. Feces can be stored here until the bird chooses to excrete it. The characteristic appearance of a bird dropping, with the white part in the middle and the green part around it, is actually the uric acid, or urine part, in the center, with the green fecal part around the outer edge.

If you own a female egg-laying cockatiel that nests on the floor of her cage, you have likely noticed that she produces a voluminous stool when you let her out of the cage. This is because during the time of nesting, many female birds will store feces in their cloaca for prolonged periods in order to not soil their nests. In the same way, many owners of hand-raised parrots have toilet trained their birds by making the bird feel that the entire home is their nest. These birds will store feces in their cloaca until the owner takes them to a suitable location and gives them the signal to defecate.

Chapter 5
Diet Basics

What Is a Balanced Diet?

One can see from the first section of the book that providing a balanced diet involves supplying carbohydrates, proteins, fats, water, and all of the essential vitamins and minerals, taking into account the effects of energy, biological availability of protein, and the possible role of fiber in your diet formulation. Simply supplying these ingredients is not enough; they must also be in correct proportion to each other to enhance their availability and decrease any negative interactions between them. Once this has been achieved, the diet must be formulated such that the bird ingests all the ingredients supplied, and does not simply select its favorites and ignore the rest. Once ingested, the diet must be able to be absorbed into the body. The diet must also be flexible, so that changes can be made according to the bird's metabolic needs during such times as stress, molt, breeding, or growth.

Achieving all this is no easy task, and major changes must take place in our perceptions of pet bird feeding in order to achieve our goal.

Why Seeds Are Not Balanced

It has been recognized for years by avian practitioners and many aviculturists that seeds are not an adequate source of nutrition in pet birds. Our discussion in the previous section has pointed out that seeds are invariably deficient in

Seeds should be fed as a treat rather than as a staple diet.

calcium, sodium, vitamins A, D_3, K, B_{12}, C, choline, and the essential amino acid lysine. Depending on the seed, riboflavin, niacin, phosphorus, iodine, copper, zinc, manganese, and selenium may also be deficient, as well as the amino acids methionine and tryptophan. Yet, even after pointing out these deficiencies, many books go on to discuss seed diets at length and simply suggest that seeds be supplemented in various ways.

If the birds ate the supplements, this approach might be adequate, but as many bird owners know, birds will continue to pick out those seeds most palatable and familiar, and ignore other seeds in the mix let alone any vegetables, fruits, or animal proteins that are provided. For this reason we must revolutionize our approach to diet formulation, and not view seeds as a basic part of the diet, but as a supplement to it.

Seeds are not poison; they need not be banned from the avian diet. On the contrary, they do contain many essential nutrients and do provide for the healthy psychological need for food manipulation by the act of hulling. It is also true that the smaller birds, such as finches and canaries, may still require a higher seed content to their diet until more is known about their dietary needs to formulate a pellet they find acceptable. However, the role of seeds in the diet must be relegated to treat feeding rather

than to a staple diet in order to meet our objective of balanced nutrition. For this reason, seeds will not be discussed at length in this section, although they will be addressed again in the chapter on specialty foods.

How Can a Balanced Diet Be Supplied?

Once we take seeds out of our perception of a staple diet, it frees up our imagination to explore many dietary alternatives. Of these alternatives, two ideas gaining wide acceptance and showing great success to date are feeding according to the four food groups, and pelleted rations. Combining these

Bread can be a source of whole grains.

methods is also widely advocated. We will discuss each method in turn.

Before we begin our discussion, however, it is important to emphasize that it is essential to read Chapter 6, Changing the Diet, before you begin attempting these new feeding regimens. It will likely decrease your level of frustration, as well as ensure a safe conversion process for your pet.

Feeding According to the Four Food Groups

This approach involves using the same four food groups that are advocated in human nutrition in order to achieve a balanced diet: grains, fruits/vegetables, meat/legumes, and dairy products. It is essential to point out that proper amounts of food from all four food groups must be eaten by the bird if a balanced diet is to be achieved.

Grains

Grains include seeds, nuts, rice, pasta, corn, cereals, and breads. This is the area in which some seed may still be used. However, it may be best not to use seeds, corn, and nuts as grain sources until the bird has been converted over to four-food-group feeding. Rice, pasta, cereals, and bread can be used in the meantime. Brown rice is preferable to white rice because the bran (brown part) of the rice kernel is the part that contains the vitamin thiamine. Pasta is often an easy item to add to the diet, because many birds love it. All pasta forms have basically the same composition as plain spaghetti, so the information provided in the charts for spaghetti can be applied to macaroni, ziti, or any other style. Using a variety of different styles emphasizes the play value of food and is a good idea. Whole wheat pastas, tomato, or spinach pastas would of course have a different composition, and I cannot make specific comments on these, except to say that vegetable pastas would likely be beneficial, particularly if the bird were not a good vegetable eater; this might be one way to sneak in some nutritive value from vegetables into the diet in a form acceptable to the bird. (Naturally it would not have as great a nutritive value as fresh vegetables would.) Corn is considered a grain in the four-food-group definition because it is high in carbohydrates and is unbalanced in its calcium:phosphorus ratio. Corn is a good source of carotenes, the precursors of vitamin A. Cereals can also be a good grain source. Choose less sweet brands such as Cheerios, Shredded Wheat, Corn Flakes, or Product 19. Many breakfast cereals have been fortified with niacin, thiamine, and riboflavin, thereby increasing their nutritive value even further. I would not suggest the use of bran-type cereals; these brands are useful to us because of the beneficial effects of fiber in our overrefined diets; as discussed in the section on fiber, your pet bird will take in enough fiber from the cereals mentioned and from fruits and vegetables to make a heavy fiber source unnecessary. From our previous discussion regarding phytic acid and minerals, it is best to choose a whole grain, yeasted bread to derive the most nutritive value. Although whole grains contain phytic acid, yeast counteracts the action of phytic acid by breaking it down. Although unleavened, matzoh and flatbreads are "fun" foods and can be used occasionally for their play value. (See Changing the Diet, Chapter 6.)

Vegetables and Fruits

Vegetables and fruits represent a large category, in that there are so many items to choose from. Remember that dark, leafy green vegetables and yellow fruits and vegetables have the best nutritive value. For this reason broccoli, carrots, squash, green beans, and red and green peppers are all good choices. Lettuce is not recommended simply because it has a high water content and not much nutritive value; so many superior choices exist. Avocados should also not be used. Although not all parts of the avocado are toxic to birds, the pit and fruit skins are, as is the brown color that seeps off the pit into the avocado flesh. Because there are so many other choices available, there is no need to use

this potentially dangerous food. Parsley has also been suggested to have toxic effects, and the reason this idea arose will be discussed further in the chapter on diet-related toxins. However, parsley in moderate amounts is not toxic to birds and can be fed.

Meats and Legumes

This group includes meats such as chicken, pork, and beef; fish such as tuna; and legumes such as kidney, lima, or pinto beans and chickpeas. Well-cooked meats and fish in small quantities can form an important nutrient source in the avian diet. I emphasize well cooked because raw meat and fish may contain pathogenic bacteria. Some people are concerned that feeding chicken meat to parrots is cannibalistic and will promote aggression. Feeding chicken meat to chickens is cannibalistic; feeding chicken meat to parrots is no more cannibalistic than feeding beef to humans. Aggression has absolutely no relationship to feeding meat. Meat is simply another form of protein, and, from our discussion on vitamins and minerals, it is an excellent source of many nutrients that are traditionally deficient in the avian diet. Many birds thoroughly enjoy dismantling a chicken thigh bone and eating the marrow. Although I would never advise giving bones to dogs and cats, a well-cooked chicken thigh bone can be given to a parrot; it is an excellent source of iron and calcium, and birds do not seem to be prone to

A well-cooked chicken thigh bone can be an excellent source of iron and calcium.

ingesting harmful bony slivers as dogs and cats are. Liver can be a good source of certain nutrients; however, it should be fed in small amounts only occasionally, no more than once a month. As discussed in the section on vitamin A, the liver is the organ responsible for detoxifying substances. For this reason, toxic environmental substances build up in the liver over time, and calf's liver is preferable to mature beef liver. The use of meat as a protein source in mynahs, toucans, aracaries, and toucanets is controversial; these species' needs will be discussed separately in another section.

Legumes are a good dietary source of protein. If canned legumes are used, they are often packed in salt water. It is important to rinse them well prior to use to avoid excess salt intake. Dried legumes can be hard to digest; they must be soaked overnight, then cooked in order to increase their nutritive value.

Dairy Products

Dairy products are a good source of calcium. Although it is true that birds lack the enzyme lac-tase needed to digest the milk sugar lactose, they seem to be able to digest small quantities of these products without developing the osmotic diarrhea one might expect. Cheese, yogurt, cottage cheese, vanilla pudding, and custard can be used in small amounts.

Eggs deserve special mention. They are an excellent source of protein and many essential nutrients, yet too much egg yolk is high in cholesterol and may have detrimental effects. Scrambled eggs, mixed with bread crumbs and fried in an iron frying pan, French toast with whole wheat bread, and pancakes are all innovative ways to add egg to the diet, and there are many others. It is my opinion that a small amount of cooked whole egg can be added to the diet once or twice a week without detrimental effect if the four-food-group method of feeding is used.

Problem Areas

The addition of a vitamin-mineral supplement to the diet is advocated with this feeding regimen. These products are discussed at greater length in the chapter on food additives.

The key to successful four-food group feeding lies in the fact that the bird must consume some of each food group each day in order to achieve a balanced diet. With some birds this can be achieved without difficulty, and the beneficial psychological effects of a stimulating, varied diet should not be underestimated, particularly in very bright birds and in birds that were originally caught in the wild.

However, some disadvantages to this feeding regimen do exist. Some birds still tend to pick out their favorite foods and do not achieve a balanced diet despite the owner's best efforts. This type of feeding regimen also involves a lot of time in food preparation. Food cannot be left in the cage for extended periods because it will spoil, leading to serious gastrointestinal infections. This makes it impossible to go away for even a day and leave the bird unattended. It is also wasteful, in that birds tend to "do the jungle-thing" and throw a piece of food to the floor after only a few bites.

These problems have led avian nutritionists to the development of a dry, homogenous, balanced ration in an effort to overcome these disadvantages. This is the reason pellets were developed.

Pellets

Over the last few years a number of different brands of pellets have been developed. For every brand on the market there are a dozen different stories of success and failure, most of them not based on scientific research, but simply on impression or hearsay. Only some brands enjoy the benefits of mass marketing. Brand loyalties tend to

be regional, and are largely based on availability; high shipping costs often make using a non-local pellet brand unpractical.

Each pellet manufacturer can state emphatically why certain ingredients are, or are not, used in their diet, and sifting through the information is a daunting task. Although no manufacturer claims to have all the answers to the questions that arise during diet formulation, they are working hard at finding them. Nutritional studies are going on at various locations around the country, and each year new information is used to upgrade the various brands. What has become apparent over the last few years is that the information that has been scientifically determined for one species may not be entirely applicable to another species, or to another stage in the growth cycle. Certain species seem to have different requirements; for example, Gloria Allen, a well-known breeder of macaws, has maintained for years

Birds often pick out their favorite foods, and don't achieve a balanced diet.

Examples of mash and two sizes of expanded pellets.

that certain species of macaws seem to need a higher fat level than is commonly recommended. Recent research has shown that her impressions may be correct.

One dietary ingredient that is controversial is the use of fish meal. Although some manufacturers maintain that fish meal has been used in the poultry industry for years without detrimental effects, others have concerns regarding the variability in the quality of certain fish meals. It has also been found that overheated fish meal can contain a component called gizzerosine, a chemical that causes ulceration of the gizzard lining by stimulating excess gastric acid secretion.

Protein levels are also controversial, but some of the variations in protein levels in the various diets can be explained. First, as discussed in the section on energy, the amount of protein actually consumed depends to a large extent on the energy level of the diet; the higher the energy level, the less of the food actually consumed, and therefore, the less actual protein consumed. Therefore, before comparing the protein levels of various diets, be sure that they are composed of comparable levels of energy. When comparing energy levels, remember that the ME, or metabolizable energy, of the diet is only an estimated figure; it may vary depending on the species of bird, or even with the method used to calculate the figure. Second, the metabolic state of the animal should also be taken into account. Tom Roudybush, an avian nutritionist, has performed feeding trials indicating that 20 percent protein is the optimum level for raising cockatiel chicks; three- to five-month-old budgerigars were found to do best on a diet of 17 percent protein, in a study done by Underwood et al, at Michigan State University; still other levels are required by other species. Protein levels required for maintenance for most species are often far lower. Traditionally, breeding birds were kept on a high-protein, breeder/grower ration all year long; a recent, more logical approach, is to supply these birds with the high-protein ration only during the time of the actual breeding cycle, when these higher levels are actually needed. Third, the digestibility of the diet must also be considered; some diets have higher digestibility than others, therefore more of the protein is biologically available to the bird.

One must also be aware of other possible oversupplementations in some diets; there is a suspicion that some formulations are too high in vitamins A, D_3, and calcium. For the same reason, vitamin and mineral supplements are not recommended for birds on pelleted diets. It is generally agreed that these diets already contain sufficient levels of these nutrients and that additional supplementation may result in overdose toxicity.

Aside from the differences in basic nutritional formulation, several other differences exist between pelleted rations. These differences include method of production, color, shape, texture, taste, and smell.

Pelleted diets are created in one of two ways. Compressed pellets are bound together by steam at high temperatures for a short period of time. These pellets often resemble pale or colored rabbit pellets, and crumble easily. They fall apart easily when mixed with water, so they are useful for making up a soft "slurry" if needed, or for mixing into a soft food diet when trying to get a bird to eat more parts of this recipe. They are also easier to break into "crumbles" to feed small or baby birds. Some people are concerned that birds cannot eat these diets well because they crumble too easily and produce more dust residues. Nonetheless,

there are many birds that prefer the texture of this type of pellet.

Expanded pellets are also bound together by high temperatures created by steam, but the cooking and drying process is much longer. These pellets have a very firm texture, do not break apart easily, and resemble dry cat food. Because of the method used in processing, it is believed that this type of formulation is less likely to have bacterial contamination, has greater digestibility, and contains less fiber. Expanded pellets that are ground into hand-feeding formulas are also less likely to settle out in the crop, a concern that is addressed at greater length in Factors of Importance in Hand-feeding, Chapter 16.

The color of the pellet varies with the manufacturer. Those manufacturers who are concerned about the possible detrimental effects of food coloring and artificial additives tend to produce a pellet that is pale yellow, green, red, or tan in color, and use naturally derived coloring agents, such as beets or chlorophyll-containing foodstuffs. Other companies argue that there are no proven detrimental effects of food coloring in pet birds, and that since birds are highly visual animals, bright colors make the food more appealing. In this case, intense shades of yellow, green, and red are chosen.

Most brands of pellets come in one shape, so that the food has a uniform appearance. Two companies have developed formulas containing several different shapes, in an effort to stimulate the bird's tactile senses as well as to add visual excitement.

Although the taste and smell of a food does not appear to be quite as important to birds as the visual and tactile nature of the diet, there is no doubt that taste and smell have an influence on diet selection. In order to fulfill this need, various companies have added natural or artificial fruit or other flavorings to increase the palatability of the diet.

Which of these factors is most important to your bird in diet selection is largely a matter of individual preference. In most cases, the answer is to experiment with several different products to find one that perks your bird's interest. Once you have discovered which diet your bird finds stimulating, you can choose other products of a similar nature and offer them as well.

There is a difference of opinion among avian veterinarians regarding whether one should stick to one brand of pellets only, or whether one should mix several brands in order to balance any excesses or deficiencies any one brand may have, because we cannot be sure at this time which formulation is best. This is a difficult question; a case can be made for either approach. I tend to lean toward mixing several brands, unless you have found a product that seems to satisfy your birds' needs completely and on which your birds appear to be thriving.

Although it would make life easier, it is impossible for me to tell you which brand of pellets is best for your particular breed of bird. However, I can make several suggestions as to what questions you should ask your particular pellet manufacturer in order to increase your confidence level in their product. What is the energy level of the diet? What is the protein level? What is the protein source used and why? Has fish meal been used, and why? What quality control measures have been used? Is there independent laboratory analysis of their food available to verify that the levels listed on the package are indeed those present in the food? What ongoing research and development are they involved in, or contributing to? (We should make an effort to support those companies involved in furthering scientific knowledge in this field.) If feeding trials have been performed, what species have been used? Is a written report of these trials available? If their levels of a certain nutrient appear higher or lower than that of a competitor, how do they justify this difference? Any reputable feed manufacturer should welcome these inquiries, and be pleased to provide the answers to your questions.

Table 5 provides a partial list of the ingredients and composition of a parrot maintenance formulation of a few of the more widely available pellet brands. This table should only be used as a general example of the kind of information a pellet manufacturer may provide or use in diet formulation; do not be tempted to compare these products directly, ignoring the points we have discussed regarding energy, biological availability of protein, and the interaction of nutritional elements within a diet.

People Food

Although feeding according to the four food groups is indeed feeding "people food," it is important to distinguish between the two. An owner who says, "My bird eats what I eat," may be providing a reasonable diet, provided the owner is nutritionally conscientious. However, if the owner only eats meat and potatoes and abhors vegetables, feeding the same diet to the bird will not result in good health. Junk food can also be a problem. The occasional french fry is tolerable, but sharing a bag of potato chips is not. Potato chips contain too high a level of salt; 3 potato chips for a small parrot would be the equivalent of 1 teaspoon of salt for a human; salt toxicity can occur, with fatal consequences.

Alcohol is detrimental to birds and should never be offered, despite some well-meaning individual's advice to the contrary. Alcohol dilates blood vessels causing an increase in heat loss in a debilitated

Unsalted popcorn is a safe treat food.

bird, and depresses the immune system. Alcohol use can also result in cirrhosis of the liver just as it does in humans.

Birds also do not need to consume heavily sugared cakes and cookies. Excess sugar in the diet may contribute to an overgrowth of a harmful yeast, Candida albicans, leading to a crop infection.

Common sense is a prerequisite in diet selection for your pet; if it isn't good for you, you can be sure it isn't good for your feathered friend either.

Other Recipes

Before pellets were developed, several aviculturists had already begun to experiment with other diets in an attempt to supply a better source of nutrition. The most famous of these is the "soft food

addition of a calcium and a vitamin and mineral supplement. This diet was widely recommended for a number of years, and is still useful today, particularly as a transition diet when trying to convert fussy eaters to pellets. A variation on this basic recipe can be found in Recipes, Chapter 10 (see page 120).

Several other innovative ideas have also been advocated, such as the "Bean-macaroni Casserole" served up by Dr. Roger Harlin to his birds, and various muffin and loaf recipes from a variety of sources. These recipes and others are described in Specialty Foods, Chapter 11 (see page 124).

diet," first advocated by Dr. Raymond Kray. This diet was a combination of equal portions of rice, corn, dog food, and legumes, such as kidney or lima beans, with the

TABLE 5
Analysis of Popular Parrot Maintenance Pellets

Analysis per kg Food	Aviary North	Hagen	Harrison's	Lake's	Mazuri	Pretty Bird	Roudybush	Topper
Me kcal/g		4.50		3.00	3.00		3.10	3.64
Crude Protein %	15.60	15.50	15.00	12.00	15.50	14.00	12.00	17.00
Crude Fat %	4.00	10.00	5.50	4.50	6.00	5.00		4.30
Crude Fiber %	3.50	4.00	2.20	5.00	3.80	4.00		6.50
Ash %					5.40			
A IU	13,200.00	16,000.00	6600.00	11,000.00	7500.00	17,600.00	11,000.00	13,785.00
D$_3$ IU	2500.00	400.00	1320.00	2640.00	1350.00	2200.00	1650.00	2970.00
E IU	121.00	220.00	8.80	66.00	125.00	330.00	18.00	105.00
K mg	3.00	2.00	3.52	154.00	3.00	2.20	5.00	.04
Thiamine mg	2.10	3.00	1.06	11.00	5.50	11.00	12.00	2.86
Riboflavin mg	10.00	7.00	.88	13.20	8.50	13.20	21.00	3.20
Niacin mg	36.00	180.00	21.12	88.00	50.00		250.00	41.36
B$_6$ mg	5.00	5.50		11.00	5.00	13.20	23.00	5.72
Pantothenic Acid mg	16.80	25.00	7.04	22.00	10.00	35.20	48.00	68.40
Biotin mcg	200.00	250.00	88.00	110.00	400.00	198.00	1000.00	180.00
Folic Acid mg	1.20	1.50	.53	2.20	2.50	2.20	4.30	5.50
B$_{12}$ mcg	16.00	18.00	17.60	44.00	25.00	44.00	30.00	222.00
Choline mg	1600.00	2250.00		1210.00	1300.00	1650.00	800.00	3454.00
C mg		200.00		154.00		176.00		3.19
Calcium %	1.50	.70	.70	.85	.85	.75	.39	1.50
Phosphorus %	.77*	.45**	.60*	.77*	.45**	.40**	.20**	.70*
Magnesium %	.23	.15	.15	.15	.16		.26	.15
Sodium %	.30	.06	.04	.18	.12	.15	.18	.07
Potassium %	.68	.40	.62	.50	.58			.64
Sulfur %		.25						.22
Manganese mg	72.00	70.00	19.00	88.00	130.00	55.00	11.50	10.00
Iron mg	72.00	200.00	65.00	154.00	140.00	75.00	280.00	130.00
Zinc mg	84.00	85.00	33.00	110.00	115.00	99.00	16.00	10.00
Copper mg	12.00	20.00		11.00	10.00	15.40	4.25	1.00
Cobalt mg					.30			
Iodine mg	.12	.50		1.54	1.00	1.40	.35	.30
Selenium mg	.12	.10		.33	.35	.20	.10	trace
Lysine %	1.40	.65		1.50	.80	.75	.53	.94
Arginine %	1.33	.87		.85		.85	.97	.98
Tryptophan %	.21	.18		.50	.17		.14	.15
Methionine %		.45		.50	.50	.50	.31	.32
Threonine %		.55		.95	.57			.59
Cystine %		.35			.26			.22

* phytate phosphorus
** non-phytate phosphorus

See Useful Literature and Addresses, page 00, for the full names and addresses of the manufacturers.

Chapter 6
Changing the Diet

Teaching an Old Bird New Tricks

Teaching a bird to accept new foods is one of the greatest challenges faced by the owner of a seed-addicted bird. Indeed, the task can be so frustrating that many articles have been written on the subject. Each author lists his or her "no-fail" methods, but the truth is that no one method will work for all birds. The secret lies in understanding what motivates your pet, and, above all, never giving up. Birds that have been eating the wrong diet for many years will not change overnight; this is hardly surprising when one considers that we humans are just as irrational. Con-

You can teach an old bird new tricks.

sider smokers who know beyond a doubt intellectually what harm smoking does to their systems, yet continue to puff away. Habit and addiction are powerful forces, and not easily overcome.

What Motivates Your Bird

In order to understand how to encourage acceptance of a new food, you must first understand a bird's natural behavior in the wild. In the wild, food gathering is one of the most important daily tasks a bird engages in. Feather maintenance, nesting, and socializing are also important activities, but all of these require energy. Because of its high metabolic rate, a bird can starve within two to three days without adequate caloric intake. Consequently food gathering takes up a large part of a bird's day, and finding new food sources is a continuous intellectual challenge and source of stimulation for the bird.

In captivity, our habit of providing the same food source located in the same position continually day after day denies the bird an important source of mental stimulation.

It is a well-known fact among those who study birds in the wild that birds are opportunistic omnivores. In other words, they will eat just about anything, as long as it meets certain criteria as far as the bird is concerned. Leaves, plants, grasses, fruits, grains, vegetables stolen from farmers' fields, nuts, roots, bulbs, insects, nectar, and sometimes clay from riverbanks, are all common food sources. The bird chooses which foods it will eat based on a number of criteria. The first criteria are previous experience and the example set by others. Beyond that, birds are attracted to food based on its physical properties. As we have discussed, eye appeal, texture, shape, smell, and size are all important factors. In effect, the decision to eat or not eat a certain food is made long before the food reaches the taste buds deep within the bird's mouth.

Because the seed diet we provide does not satisfy the bird completely, displacement behavior occurs. The natural instinctive behavior of the bird is thwarted by the artificial environment we provide. When a normal response to a situation cannot occur, an abnormal response does. This response is called a displacement behavior. Feather picking is a classic displacement behavior that is common in captivity and is not seen in the wild. Sunflower seed "addiction" is also a classic displacement behavior, and is one of the most common conditions seen in daily avian pet practice. Sunflower seeds are not "addictive" per se; contrary to popular belief, it has been shown that they do not contain any addictive substances. Sunflower seed "addiction" relates more to the powerful psychological reward that cracking these seeds provides rather than to any substance contained within them.

It is obvious, then, that the common methods of feeding do not provide suitable motivation for our pet birds, nor does simply placing a new food in the cage provide the motivation the bird requires to eat it. Motivation can only be stimulated by renewing your bird's interest in food as a source of pleasure.

Feather picking is a common displacement behavior.

How to Renew Your Bird's Interest

Before you can even begin to introduce new foods, you must first reestablish food as a source of interest for your bird. In the wild, most food gathering activity takes place at dusk and at dawn. Thus, the very first thing you need to do is to establish a twice daily feeding schedule. A bird can fill its crop in 15 to 60 minutes, and this quantity of food will last 8 to 12 hours, so you needn't worry about your bird starving during the day. However, I will add that common sense dictates that you must provide food twice daily on a consistent basis, and not forget to come home one night and miss a feeding altogether. It is also true that very small species of birds, such as finches and canaries, cannot go this long between feedings, and a minimum of three meals a day are required.

Twice daily feeding has several important psychological benefits. It increases hunger, and therefore the desire for food that has been previously blunted by ready availability. It increases bonding between you and your pet, because your pet begins to recognize you as the food source. It prevents boredom by creating a mental state of anticipation. It also has the psychological benefit of allowing the bird to feed in a group if you make a point of eating your own meals at the same time in the presence of the bird, because birds are group feeders.

How to Introduce New Foods

Once this pattern has been established, many methods of new food introduction can be tried. The important thing to remember is that birds are always suspicious of anything new, so that a new food must be presented consistently several days in a row before you can even hope to have it noticed. Birds also have changes in taste just as we do; they can also become bored with certain foods, and go off them for a while, only to enjoy them again several weeks or months later.

The following is a list of several successful methods of new food introduction. Experimentation will help you choose the method best suited to your pet.

During the day, put only some of the new food in the food bowl, not the regular diet. If your bird gets hungry during the day, it may venture trying it.

Place a thin layer of the new food over the top of the regular diet so the bird has to pick through it to get to the known food. Make sure you sprinkle the new food over the top in front of the bird, so that the bird knows that there is something it considers edible underneath, or the bird may refuse to touch the food altogether. In this way the bird becomes familiar with the new food, even though it will likely just fling it to the side to begin with in its search for the "tried and true."

Mix the new diet in with the regular diet in a ratio of 10 percent new diet to 90 percent regular food. Over the course of several weeks, gradually increase the new food by 10 percent increments each week until you have completely converted to the new food. This method is especially successful with soft food diet conversion and pelleted feeds. Some birds will balk at the 50 percent level, as though they have figured out what you are doing, and are asserting their will like any petulant two-year-old. Screaming bouts can occur, and some birds will tip over their food dish and refuse to eat altogether. If this occurs, back off by 10 percent for one week, then gradually increase again. Usually they don't notice the second time around.

Some foods are almost universally acceptable and therefore make a good starting point for a new food introduction. Many birds are familiar with corn even in the wild from raiding farmers' fields, so corn is often an acceptable food source. Once the corn has been accepted, other foods can sometimes be mixed with creamed corn.

If the bird is particularly people oriented, sometimes the best trick is to eat the new food in front of it. Make loud noises of approval, widen your eyes in an effort to mimic the bird's ability to dilate its pupils when excited, and make every effort to imply how wonderful the new treat is. The first time you do this, refuse to share your treat, even if your bird comes over to ask for it. Repeat this two or three days in a row. Most birds will be begging for a taste after a few days. They

Eating in front of your bird may encourage it to try new foods.

Many birds enjoy food they can grasp with their foot.

may grab the food and fling it to the floor, but continue with your charade of how wonderful it is. Few birds can resist this routine for long.

If your bird is "pair-bonded" with one member of the family, have another member of the family hand-feed the human the bird is pair-bonded to. The person receiving the treat should go through the same routine of enjoyment. Place the bird on a perch directly between the two people, so that the food is literally passed under the bird's nose on the way to the other human's mouth. Hand-raised babies cannot resist this method.

It is always easier to introduce a new diet to a group of birds rather than to a single bird. Competition for food is a powerful motivating factor for some species. Seeing a bird of their flock trying something new definitely increases its acceptability to other members of the flock.

Color can be an important component of food acceptability. Remember that birds have excep-

tionally keen eyesight. If your bird eats cherries but refuses sweet potatoes, sometimes adding a drop of red food coloring will do the trick.

Texture is also an important component of food acceptability. If your bird doesn't like raw vegetables, try them cooked and mashed. Some birds prefer crumbly pellets, whereas other birds prefer the firmer extruded kind.

Size is also an important criterion. Just as some birds won't eat certain seeds because they are too large to hull, some foods may need to be cut into a size more acceptable. Many parrots, particularly Amazons, prefer food they can grasp in their foot and hold while they eat a little at a time. Carrot sticks and green beans may be accepted for this reason.

Smell can also be a motivating factor. If your bird hates mashed potatoes but likes bananas, adding a few drops of banana extract to the potatoes will give off a wonderful fragrance that may make the potatoes acceptable.

Varying color, size, and texture uses the bird's natural preferences to help in a diet transition; taste can also be used in this way. As mentioned previously, the flavors of hot peppers, marjoram, onion, and paprika seem to be favored by some birds. If your bird likes cheese, a little Cheez Whiz (Kraft) can be poured over broccoli or mixed with other foods to increase their appeal.

Changing the Diet Safely

Essential to any diet conversion technique is patience and keen observation of your pet. Conversion through starvation is a totally unacceptable approach under any circumstances. If your bird drops more than 10 percent of its body weight, reassess your technique and try another approach once its weight is back up to normal. Some birds would literally rather starve than switch if they are forced into making a diet change too quickly.

If you do not have the ability to weigh your bird at home, other options are available. Discuss setting up a twice weekly weigh-in with your avian veterinarian if you are making a complete diet transition. A technician can weigh the bird and notify the veterinarian if an unacceptable weight loss is occurring.

A change in attitude, condition, or droppings is also an important clue for determining how the diet change is going. If the bird is fluffed, listless, or sitting on the floor of the cage, a problem should be suspected. The keel bone, which is the bone that runs down the center of the bird's chest, should be well fleshed, like the breast of a chicken. If the keel bone is becoming too prominent, excessive weight loss is occurring.

Before beginning any diet change, monitor the number of droppings your bird normally pro-

If your bird becomes fluffed or listless, a problem should be suspected.

duces in a day. (For example, budgies produce an average of 18 to 24 droppings in a 24-hour period.) Count the number of droppings produced again once you have switched to twice daily feeding. There should be little or no difference between these two numbers. Then count the number of droppings produced when you change the diet or introduce new foods. A decrease of 20 percent in the number of droppings once you have begun the new food may be excessive and should be investigated further. A very dark green or black stool can indicate the bird is not eating, and is a cause for concern. I will add one caution against developing what I call "poop paranoia"; certainly a change in diet will cause some change in the nature of the droppings. A mild variation in the color of the dropping from one shade of green to another, a slight change in bulk, or a mild change in moisture content is not a cause for panic; if you think the change is excessive, save the droppings, and consult your avian veterinarian. This advice applies to the fecal portion of the stool. The urate or urine portion of the stool is another matter; this is the white portion of the stool and it should stay consistently white. If the urate portion becomes very watery, or becomes yellow or yellow-green in color, it may indicate excessive metabolism of body tissues or illness and should be investigated immediately.

Food As a Source of Pleasure

An interesting and varied diet has many emotional benefits for your pet.

Once you have retrained your bird to eat a variety of new foods and have reawakened its senses,

continue to use food as a source of pleasure and enjoyment. Sally Blanchard, an avian enthusiast, pet bird consultant, writer, regular contributor to *Bird Talk* magazine, and the editor of the *Pet Bird Report,* has a number of wonderful suggestions on ways to make food interesting for your pet. She maintains that play is an important part of the feeding ritual and should be encouraged. Food that can be unwrapped, such as peas and beans, grapes that can be peeled, corn on the cob, kiwi fruit, or oranges all have an enormous appeal. Texture can add its own fascination; broccoli, cauliflower, or carrots cut into curlicues or flower shapes, can fulfill this need. As Ms. Blanchard says, "In the wild, food does not appear in cups strategically placed on tree branches. Parrots have to reach, climb and explore to eat." (*Bird Talk*, April 1991). Hanging food from the center of the cage and hiding treats in paper towel rolls, paper bags, pitas, or tortillas are all wonderful ways to stimulate your bird, not to mention stretching your own imagination a little to come up with new ideas.

A word of caution should be added regarding how to secure foods in the cage. Shower curtain hooks are easily opened by parrots and should never be used; I have seen several cases of birds impaled on these, hanging from their jaw, and frantically trying to free themselves. String can become wrapped around toes or legs, acting as a tourniquet. Leather thongs can be used fairly safely, as can "quick-links" (available in hardware stores). Your local pet store may also carry a selection of clips that can be used for this purpose. If you have a large parrot, be sure to choose a clip that the bird cannot dismantle and swallow accidentally.

The psychological importance of adding fun and excitement to your approach to feeding your pet bird cannot be overemphasized. The emotional benefits to the bird are tremendous, as is the pleasure you can derive from watching your pet explore its environment with a renewed interest.

Chapter 7
Diet and Disease

This section will review a number of disease conditions that are recognized to have a dietary origin, or which can be improved through correct dietary management. However, even more important than an understanding of individual diseases is an understanding of the fundamental relationship between diet and disease.

Throughout our discussion on vitamins, minerals, and amino acids, we have seen the profound effects different deficiencies and excesses can have on the body. What we have not discussed much as yet is the importance of these various elements in the functioning of the immune system.

Many studies have been performed with poultry in an effort to determine the importance of various nutrients in the function of the immune system. Although this is not yet confirmed through research, it is likely that these elements have similar effects on pet birds. For example, deficiencies in the amino acids methionine, valine, or threonine will suppress the immune system; excess dietary methionine or cysteine will have the same effect. Defi-ciencies in the minerals copper, chlorine, iron, sodium, and selenium will also have a suppressive effect, as will excesses in chlorine. Vitamins A, D, E, riboflavin, pyridoxine, pantothenic acid, folacin, and vitamin B_{12} will also cause immunosuppression if fed in deficient quantities. Interestingly, mildly excessive levels of vitamins A and E may stimulate the immune response.

The various ways in which these elements exert these effects on the body are complex, and it is not necessary for us to discuss them in order to appreciate the meaning of these findings; they simply serve to further illustrate the complexity of the factors that need to be taken into account in diet formulation. For example, as mentioned, we know that methionine is an important amino acid in the functioning of the immune system. Yet, in commercial diets formulated with corn and soybean meal as the primary protein sources, methionine is the "first limiting" amino acid. In other words, methionine is the first amino acid that becomes deficient in a corn-soybean meal-based diet, depending on whether the bird's requirements are increased or if the protein level in the diet is decreased. Oversupplementing with methionine to compensate for this is not beneficial; excess levels of methionine are as immunosuppressive as deficiencies are.

Aside from the direct effects of dietary deficiencies, diseases of the digestive tract can interfere dramatically with the absorption of nutrients from the gastrointestinal tract. For example, tapeworm infestation, not uncommon in wild-caught African gray parrots, can result in a thin, unthrifty bird, due to chronic malabsorption. Giardia, a common intestinal parasite in California and in many other areas, also results in malabsorption, as do a number of other intestinal parasites in birds. Diseases of the liver or pancreas can also cause malabsorption of certain nutritional elements, either due to a lack of digestive enzymes needed to break down the nutrient into a metabolizable form, or due to an inability to assimilate the element because of organ dysfunction.

These points serve to illustrate the overall effect of diet on disease. The diseases below illustrate the importance of individual elements in certain disease processes.

The Importance of Good Hygiene

The importance of good nutrition has been established; equally important in disease prevention is proper food management to prevent bacterial contamination.

Disease prevention is always easier and less expensive than disease management, yet there is something about human nature that drives us to neglect the most fundamental principles until it's almost too late. This principle also applies to how we handle food, but it is my hope that by reviewing some of these basic principles you will be less likely to make these food handling errors.

Disease is never a spontaneous occurrence; two conditions must always be present in order for disease to occur. First, the bird must be susceptible to the illness, and second, the bird must be exposed to the object or condition that causes the illness. For example, you can't die from falling off a building unless you actually fall. In the same

Never feed birds from your mouth; our normal bacterial flora contains many organisms that are pathogenic for birds.

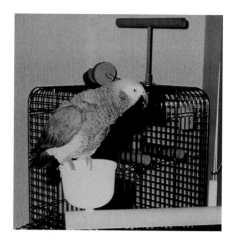

way, a bird cannot become ill from a pathogenic (disease-causing) bacteria or yeast, unless it is actually exposed to the bacteria or yeast. By practicing proper hygiene, you minimize the chances that the bird will be exposed to a disease-causing agent.

Bacteria and yeast are not spontaneous; they have to come from somewhere. Even then, they have to be given the conditions that allow them to grow to levels that will cause disease. It is virtually impossible for us to completely prevent the occurrence of all bacteria and yeast in our environment. These organisms are everywhere, and unless you were to sterilize food by prolonged heating (a process that would destroy most of its nutritive value) it is virtually impossible to avoid some contamination of the food. For this reason, it is important that the immune system functions well in order to combat this food contamination.

Birds, like all animals, do have a pretty good immune system, and when they are in good health and not stressed by conditions of poor nutrition, molt, growth, old age, or disease, they can fight off many of the pathogenic organisms they encounter. However, when they are immune-compromised by any of the stress conditions just mentioned, their ability to combat illness is decreased; at this time, exposure to even low levels of organisms can cause illness. This is why stress prevention is important in disease prevention, and why it is important for you to consult with your avian veterinarian on how to minimize the effects of these stress conditions.

Even when the immune system is functioning well, it is possible to expose a bird to levels of bacteria or yeast that can overwhelm its immune system. Although we do not have much control over the presence of low levels of bacteria and yeast in the food, we do have control over the presence of high levels of these contaminants by not providing conditions that stimulate their growth.

Pathogenic bacteria and yeast can be ingested from three sources: contaminated food, contaminated water, or a contaminated environment.

Pathogens from Food

Food can be contaminated in a number of ways. First, even commercially-produced packaged diets can sometimes harbor pathogenic organisms. Therefore, always purchase a good quality product from a company with high standards of quality control, and never feed a product whose packaging appears damaged, or that has gone past its expiration date. Second, food can be contaminated by careless handling and poor hygiene. Humans harbor several bacteria that are harmless to us but that are pathogenic for birds. It is important to wash your hands before handling your bird's food, and to never offer a bird food from your mouth. Third, food bowls can be contaminated by feces, spoiled food, or by excess moisture that allows the bacteria to multiply rapidly. It is important to place food and water cups up off the floor and out from under perches so the bird cannot inadvertently soil the food cup.

Some birds like to sleep on the edge of their food cup, and inadvertently soil it overnight. There are two ways one can prevent this. Often birds sleep on the edge of their food cup because it is the highest "perch" in their cage, and provides a sense of security for the bird. (For most birds, the higher the perch, the safer they feel.) In this case, providing a perch that is higher, located away from the food bowl, and of a comfortable diameter for a firm grip, will stop this behavior. In other cases, using a bowl that hangs outside the cage so that there is only an enclosed feeding port that the bird has access to is the correct solution. It is best if the enclosed feeding port is of wire or clear plastic; some cages have been designed with a dark plastic or opaque enclosure. Many birds are afraid of this and are reluctant to put their heads into what is, in their perception, a "dark hole."

Virtually any food will spoil if left in the cage too long. Bacteria such as the pathogenic organism E. coli can multiply every 15 minutes, doubling its density each time. Fruits, vegetables, and moist foods should only be left in the cage for a few hours. At that time, the dish must be taken out and disinfected as thoroughly (if not more) as you would your own dishes. Sometimes two, or even three, sets of dishes are practical so that you can always provide clean dishes, even if you don't have time at that moment to thoroughly disinfect one set.

Even dry foods can become contaminated. Gravity feeders are practical in that often they have a smaller feeding surface that decreases the surface contamination of the food, but people often make the mistake of just filling from the top and not inspecting the feeding tray. The feeding tray can often be contaminated by the buildup of old or moist food in the corners, either because of the bird's habit of always eating out of one side of the cup, or by moisture from saliva or water seeping into the corners causing the food to cake there.

Food can also spoil before it is placed in the cage if it is improperly stored. Frozen foods can be contaminated if the time involved in thawing the food is long enough to allow bacteria to multiply. Moist foods such as the soft food diet can be stored in plastic "baggies" in individual portions, and thawed quickly in the microwave as needed to decrease the time involved in the freeze/thaw process. Dry foods should always be stored in closed containers in a cool, dry, dark place. Closed containers prevent contamination by vermin, such as mice or bugs, and help to prevent oxidation of the food by decreasing the exposure to air. Large portions of dry food can be stored in moisture-proof containers in the freezer, with only a small portion of food being left out for daily use. Never dip a used food dish into the main food container; always use a clean scoop to move food from the storage container to the dish to avoid contaminating the main food source with the dirty dish.

Pathogens from Water

Water can also be contaminated with pathogenic organisms. Open

Poor food dish placement can result in contamination with fecal waste.

water dishes are exposed to contamination from particles in the air or from feces. For this reason, a small-mouthed gravity waterer is preferred, or a sipper-tube can be used if the bird is taught how to use it. (Position the sipper tube so that the bird is not able to chew the rubber stopper.) It is important to change the water at least once a day, and to clean the waterer thoroughly to prevent bacterial buildup. The water source can also be contaminated. Many water pipes (particularly those made from PVC) can harbor bacteria that can multiply tremendously between faucet uses. For this reason, be sure to run the water for two minutes before filling the bird's waterer, or boil the water before use. Remember to inspect and clean the screen in your faucet from time to time.

Pathogens from the Environment

Birds can also ingest pathogenic bacteria from the environment; because birds tend to use their beak as a third foot, they are continuously mouthing the bars and perches as they make their way around their cage. If the bars and perches are soiled with spoiled food or feces, the bird is exposed to high levels of pathogenic bacteria. The floor of the cage can be a source of contamination, even if the bird doesn't go down to it very often; particles of dried feces can aerosolize and contaminate food and water dishes. For this reason, cage cleanliness cannot be overemphasized. It is important to wash the entire cage thoroughly at least once a week with a good quality disinfectant, as well as to change the cage bottom daily. Your avian veterinarian can suggest disinfectants that are suitable for your dishes and for the bird's cage.

Testing for Pathogens

If you are in doubt about the bacterial levels in your food or water sources, your avian veterinarian can perform a test called a "culture and sensitivity." Samples can be taken from food or water sources and analyzed for their levels of bacterial contamination. This procedure is somewhat expensive, but is more than worth the cost if it helps eliminate a serious potential disease source. For example, one large breeding facility was experiencing an unusually high number of Pseudomonas bacterial infections in their baby birds. A culture and sensitivity test of their water sources showed that the Pseudomonas organism was growing in their well water and brooder water.

Candidiasis

Candidiasis refers to the disease condition caused by the organism Candida albicans. Candida albicans is a yeastlike organism that is common in the environment and is often present in the crop in very low numbers, but certain conditions predispose the bird to an overgrowth of this organism, resulting in disease. The disease can affect any age group, but the causes and appearance of the disease vary somewhat depending on which age group is involved.

Candidiasis is common in baby birds, particularly in environments where proper sanitation and hygiene practices are not followed. The organism proliferates in wet and dirty nest boxes, dirty incubators and brooders, improperly stored and prepared foods, and improperly sanitized hand-feeding equipment. Parent birds can also transmit it to their offspring when feeding. The organism generally forms lesions in the upper digestive tract, so that it may involve the oropharynx, the esophagus, the crop, the proventriculus, and the gizzard. The most commonly recognized site of infection is the crop. Signs of a crop infection in baby birds include delayed crop emptying, a foul odor, vomiting, stunting, failure to thrive, and a thickened crop wall. Small ulcerative lesions may also be seen at the angles of the beak. In severe cases the crop lining may take on almost a terryclothlike appearance.

In adult birds the infection can be caused by prolonged antibiotic therapy that tends to wipe out the normal bacterial flora so that the yeast are able to proliferate. Or it may be caused by an unsanitary environment or by any condition that weakens the immune system so that it is less able to resist the organism, such as a heavy molt or a poor level of nutrition. In adult birds vomiting is a common sign of a crop infection, as is a thickened crop wall and an increase in mucus production. Candida can also cause ulcerative lesions in the oropharynx. These lesions are extremely painful, so that the bird becomes reluctant to eat, resulting in weight loss and death if it remains untreated.

Your avian veterinarian can easily diagnose this disease by taking samples from a lesion, a crop wash, or a fecal sample, staining it, and looking at it under the microscope for the characteristic budding yeast appearance.

The treatment regimen your avian veterinarian will choose will depend somewhat on the age of the bird, the severity of the infec-

Vomit on the head feathers of a budgerigar; vomiting can be a sign of a crop infection.

tion, and your ability to treat the bird adequately. In some cases the bird may need to be hospitalized and treated until it is stable enough to continue treatment at home. Do not underestimate the severity of a crop infection; left untreated it is a life-threatening condition.

Psittacine Proventricular Dilatation Syndrome

Psittacine proventricular dilatation syndrome was first recognized in the 1970s in macaws, and was tentatively referred to as "Macaw Wasting Disease" for lack of a better term. Since then it has been seen in many pet bird species including cockatoos, conures, mini-macaws, and eclectus parrots, and has been renamed in order to provide a more accurate description of the condition.

The condition is characterized by regurgitation, passing of whole seeds in the droppings, diarrhea, secondary bacterial infections, depression, progressive weight loss, and death. Some birds may also show signs related to the central nervous system, such as incoordination, abnormal head movements, or lameness. The most common finding internally is that the proventriculus is dilated and unable to contract properly, so that the food sits in the digestive tract and is not moved through properly.

The cause of the disease is not yet known, although it is believed to be caused by a virus that selectively destroys the nervous system tissue of the proventriculus, gizzard, and the small intestine. Once these nerves are destroyed they cannot regrow, so that the damage to the intestinal tract is permanent. The damaged intestinal tract can no longer function properly, and this predisposes it to secondary bacterial and yeast infection, because the food is not moved through the digestive tract properly.

There is no specific treatment for this condition, and, to date, most affected birds do eventually die. Tom Roudybush, an avian nutritionist, has developed a nutritious, highly digestible diet that can be fed and that appears to be better absorbed, thereby helping to slow down the weight loss that is characteristic of the disease; however, it does not cure the condition. There are rare cases that have shown some clinical improvement on some treatment regimens, but whether these birds have actually recovered, or whether they will relapse, is unknown.

Although there is a lot of research currently underway regarding this condition, no treatment or vaccine against it is yet available. For this reason, the best protection against this disease at this time is to prevent the condition from getting into your group of birds in the first place by having an adequate quarantine period. Two months is a minimum time frame, and six months is even better.

Feather Abnormalities

Feather abnormalities are extremely common in pet birds, and have a variety of causes. One of the most frequent abnormalities recognized by owners is a condition characterized by a loss of pigment in the feathers, such that feathers that would normally be green, for example, appear to be black. In some species the black appearance is not characteristic; in these species another color may develop. For example, Lutino cockatiels may develop feathers that are too bright a shade of yellow, and African gray parrots may develop too many red feathers. For the sake of simplicity, I have grouped all of these abnormalities under one heading to show how these various abnormalities are likely to have similar causes.

One of the major causes of feather abnormalities in most species is malnutrition. When one considers that 10 percent of the body weight is feathers, and that most birds are deficient in several of the essential nutrients that form feathers, it is easy to see that this statement is correct. Some of the nutrients that are commonly

deficient and that can have an effect on feather appearance are lysine, methionine, riboflavin, choline, and calcium. Signs of nutritional deficiency are related to an inability to produce new feathers, resulting in too long a period between molts, or in an actual weakness in the construction of the feather itself because of a lack of proper "building blocks," such as essential amino acids during the time of feather construction. Poor feather construction will result in a

feather that wears out in a few months of regular preening, as opposed to lasting the year it normally should. Poor feather construction may also cause it to reflect light differently, so that the feather color changes. Abnormal yellow feathers in cockatiels are also often identified with liver disease in this species, which may be caused by a variety of things, including poor nutrition.

There are also other causes of poor feather quality that should be addressed. Psittacine Beak and Feather Disease (PBFD) is a disease common in cockatoos, although it is also seen in many other pet bird species. The first signs that may be seen in cockatoos may only be a loss of powder down, resulting in a shiny beak and a less powdery appearance to the feathers. Eventually the disease progresses to feather loss, clubbed feathers, an excessively long beak and toenails, and, eventually, death. This disease is caused by a contagious virus, and it is important to consult with your avian veterinarian to rule out this disease if you are seeing these signs, before presuming the cause of the distorted feathers is just dietary.

Handling your birds excessively will also damage their feather quality. I have many hand-raised babies in my practice who have poor feather quality not because of their diet, which is well balanced, but because of their owners. Because these birds tend to be sitting on their owners a lot, these birds are stroked almost continuously. The natural oils from our hands, to say nothing of makeup and hand lotions, greases the feathers and gives them a ratty appearance.

A less common manifestation of feather picking called overpreening will also destroy feather quality. Unlike the typical feather picker, which pulls out the entire feather or bites it off at the base, these birds simply mouth their feathers excessively until they damage the feather by excessive manipulation.

Even normal feathers wear out over time if too long a period elapses between molts. Signs of wear include a dull, drab appearance or blackened and frayed edges. The molt can be delayed because of malnutrition, but may also be delayed if the bird is under a condition of continual stress, such as an underlying disease problem or a psychologically stressful environment.

I would not advise the use of any of the grooming products and feather sprays available on the market. These products interfere with the normal feather-protective substances the bird produces, thereby defeating their purpose. The best feather maintenance product you can apply to your bird is a daily misting of plain warm water (provided the bird can dry off in a warm, draft-free environment afterward).

The essential point to remember is that a bird's feather condition is an

Two examples of psittacine beak and feather disease.

outward manifestation of its inner condition. If your bird suffers from poor feather quality, it is important to have its entire health status assessed before starting on a regimen of unbalanced dietary supplements. As we have discussed throughout the book, the balance of the nutrients provided is as important as any one nutrient itself. For this reason, it is important to improve the entire nutritional status of the bird rather than to just oversupplement any one element.

Hypocalcemia in a dove resulting in beak deformity.

Hypocalcemia

Hypocalcemia means a lack of calcium in the bloodstream. Because calcium is involved in many essential metabolic processes, signs of calcium deficiency vary greatly depending on the degree of hypocalcemia, the age group, the species, and the reproductive state of the bird.

Mild calcium deficiency may result in nonspecific signs: prolonged blood-clotting time, poor feather quality, thin eggshells, and an unthrifty type of bird. More advanced calcium deficiency will result in egg binding, rickets, osteomalacia, and secondary nutritional hyperparathyroidism. We will discuss each of these conditions in turn.

Egg Binding

Despite many theories on the causes of egg binding over the years, it has become increasingly evident that the most common cause of egg binding is hypocalcemia. Some females can produce several clutches of eggs successfully in spite of a diet deficient in calcium, because they draw on their own body reserves in order to produce a healthy egg. Sooner or later, however, this reserve of calcium is depleted, and egg binding occurs.

Clinical signs of egg binding include weakness, a fluffed appearance, evidence of straining, and a swollen abdomen (although in some cases a swollen abdomen may not be evident if the egg is high up in the oviduct). A history of nesting activity or previous egg production is usually present. Palpating the abdomen may reveal the presence of a hard mass, which is the egg, although this may be difficult to feel if the egg is soft-shelled, and a radiograph may be needed to confirm the diagnosis. Most birds are unable to defecate because the egg obstructs the cloaca and compresses the ureters of the kidneys. This allows a buildup of toxic wastes in the system, and is one of the major causes of death in this condition.

The egg becomes "stuck" in the oviduct because of one of several reasons: lack of normal muscle tone and insufficient lubrication (both under calcium control) may prevent the delivery of even a normal-shelled egg; misshapen eggs resulting from insufficient calcium in their shell are even more likely to be a problem; soft-shelled eggs are difficult to propel down the oviduct, as are eggs that are too large or deformed.

Egg binding is a life-threatening condition that requires immediate veterinary intervention. Injections of calcium are given, followed by drugs to stimulate contractions of the uterus. If these are unsuccessful, the egg may be manually or surgically manipulated to aid in its passage. In some cases, a cesarean section or a hysterectomy must be performed in order to remove the egg.

Rickets

Rickets is a term used to describe a skeletal disease seen in young, growing birds. It more correctly refers to a lack of vitamin D_3 in the diet, but because the lack of vitamin D_3 results in improper calcium homeostasis, it has been included in this section for the sake of simplicity. The problem occurs when the areas that need to be mineralized for normal skeletal growth, namely the growth cartilage matrix and the new bone intercellular material, fail to be mineralized properly. This results in stunted growth, curved long bones, pathological fractures, and abnormal or impaired healing of those fractures. These birds have splayed legs, soft beaks, and a "runty" appearance. "Rachitic rosary" refers to the swelling and appearance of "beading" of the rib heads, a common feature of the disease.

Rickets must be treated promptly with proper vitamin and mineral supplementation, or the bony changes that have occurred cannot be reversed and the bird is permanently crippled. It is essential not to oversupplement, particularly with vitamin D_3, or you may be trading one disease for another. (See Table 3.)

Osteomalacia

Osteomalacia refers to the same process as rickets, but in the adult bird. Because cartilage growth has ceased, the disease causes a decreased concentration of calcium and phosphorus in the bone matrix only. The cortices of the bones are thickened, but are composed of fragile fibrous connective tissue that fractures easily. The sternum (breastbone) and rib cage are soft, and the sternum may actually curve. Soft-shelled eggs, egg binding, and decreased hatchability can also occur.

Osteomalacia is a common condition in chronic egg layers, especially chronic egg laying budgerigars, cockatiels, and lovebirds. In some cases, even proper dietary supplementation with vitamin D_3 and calcium cannot compensate for the rate of egg production in these birds. A normal bird produces roughly two clutches of four eggs per year. Many chronic egg layers produce several dozens of eggs per year, with few, if any, rest cycles in between production. In these cases egg production must be halted in order to give the body time to recuperate and replenish its mineral reserves before the next cycle. Your avian veterinarian can advise you on natural and hormonal ways egg production can be stopped. In some cases, a hysterectomy is the only way to stop a bird from killing itself through excessive egg production.

Secondary Nutritional Hyperparathyroidism

The parathyroid gland is responsible for maintaining serum levels of calcium. If calcium deficiency is long-term, the parathyroid gland will undergo a process called hyperplasia (excess growth) as a compensatory mechanism for maintaining plasma calcium levels. This condition is called secondary nutritional hyperparathyroidism, which simply means excess parathyroid growth secondary to dietary causes.

Excess production of the parathyroid hormone results in symptoms such as excess thirst, decreased appetite, regurgitation, weakness, and hypocalcemic tetanic (contracted or rigid) seizures.

This disease is not only caused by calcium deficiency, but also by excessively high levels of dietary phosphorus that suppresses calcium absorption. This disease can be prevented and reversed by proper dietary management of the calcium:phosphorus ratio.

Hypocalcemia Syndrome of African Grays

The African gray parrot species are often afflicted with a syndrome characterized by low serum calcium levels and convulsions. The condition most often affects Congo and Timneh African grays between the ages of two and five. Studies have shown that these species may not be able to metabolize calcium from their skeleton in times of increased need. Because they cannot access a skeletal reserve, a diet low in calcium may result in acutely low blood calcium levels and tetanic seizures caused by the hypocalcemia. Death can occur during one of these tetanic episodes. Postmortem findings have revealed enlarged, degenerative parathyroid glands, though the cause of the degeneration is not known.

For this reason, careful monitoring of dietary calcium levels and additional calcium supplementation have been recommended in these species.

Conure Bleeding Syndrome

An unusual bleeding disorder has been recognized in conures, characterized by recurrent bleeding episodes. The bone marrow diagnosis of the disease is usually erythremic myelosis (a problem in the bone marrow production of red blood cells). It has been found that the birds affected with this condition have consistently low blood calcium levels. It is also known that vitamin K deficiency causes prolonged clotting time, anemia, and hemorrhage in many tissues. Prolonged clotting time has been found to respond to vitamin K injections, even where vitamin K deficiency has not been confirmed.

For these reasons, calcium supplementation, along with vitamin K supplementation, is often used to try to prevent or decrease the frequency and/or severity of the bleeding episodes. This approach has had some success with this condition, though the exact cause of this syndrome has yet to be determined.

Hemochromatosis

Hemochromatosis is also called "iron storage disease." It occurs as result of excess storage of iron in various body tissues, including the liver. It is common in mynahs, birds of paradise, and toucans, but has also been reported in a number of other species, including cockatoos. Signs of the disease include labored breathing, muscle wasting, and a swollen abdomen often distended with fluid (ascites).

As already discussed in the chapter on vitamins and minerals, iron is absorbed by cells in the intestinal mucosa. When enough iron is present, a "mucosal block" is formed, and iron is no longer absorbed but excreted in the feces. In hemochromatosis, iron absorption is not regulated, and more iron than needed is absorbed and stored. How and where this failure of proper iron metabolism occurs in the body is not known, and is an area of current research.

The disease is mentioned here because many people have postulated a dietary cause of the condition. Recent research has not been able to confirm diet as a cause of this condition; this disease has been seen in birds on a diet that would normally be considered to contain regular levels of iron. Tom Roudybush believes that conditions such as stress, lead toxicosis, coccidiosis, and fasting followed by gorging may be more likely to result in this disease than excessive dietary iron levels. In spite of this, some lesions similar to this disease have been induced experimentally in pigeons on a diet excessively high in iron, so that the idea that the original source of the excess iron may be from excessive intestinal absorption has not been ruled out yet. It is also known that many of the commercially available mynah bird diets contain high levels of iron when compared to iron requirements in poultry.

Recent research has involved feeding diets restricted in their iron content to see whether the disease could be prevented or controlled in susceptible species. Preliminary

Toucans are prone to hemachromatosis.

results have shown some promise, so that if you own a susceptible species it may be wise to consult with your avian veterinarian to see how this research is progressing, and whether an iron-restricted diet is warranted for your pet bird.

In humans, it is known that choline or folic acid deficiency accompanying excess levels of iron will aggravate the disease. I suspect that we may discover that these two elements may also be important in this disease in birds as well.

Hypovitaminosis A

Vitamin A deficiency is one of the most commonly recognized vitamin deficiencies in pet birds. Although vitamin A is known to have effects on vision and skeletal development, it is due to its effects on epithelial maintenance that signs of deficiency are most often recognized.

The epithelial effects of vitamin A deficiency depend on the location and type of epithelial tissue

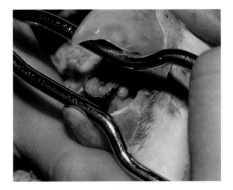

A sterile abscess caused by hypovitaminosis A.

involved. If the tissue involved is squamous epithelium (like the tissue of the mouth or skin), the major effect is a thickening of the keratin layer, causing excess keratin production. If the tissue involved is non-squamous epithelium (like the upper respiratory tract, kidney tubules, or ureters), the tissue will change to squamous tissue, resulting in excess squama production followed by excess keratin production.

Early cases of vitamin A deficiency may be recognized by blunted choanal papillae, dry eyes and thickened third eyelids, sneezing and sinusitis, poor feather quality, and a tendency toward rough scaly skin, corns, and bumblefoot. Reproductive failure in the form of impaired sperm formation, soft-shelled eggs, and weakened embryos may also occur.

Severe cases result in sterile abscesses filled with keratin of the glands in the mouth, labored respiration due to excessive squamous growth in the syrinx (part of the trachea), and swollen sinuses. Renal gout may occur because of excessive squamous growth of the kidney tubules and ureters resulting in a backup of uric acid and urates.

Treatment in severe cases may require vitamin A injections until dietary improvement can be instituted. Thankfully, most of the lesions of vitamin A deficiency can be reversed with proper dietary supplementation if the disease is caught in time.

Sinusitis

Sinusitis is a common problem in pet birds, particularly in African gray and Amazon parrots. The sinuses form bony cavities in the skull, and communicate with one another and the nose through very narrow passages, sometimes no wider than a few millimeters across. Mucus normally circulates freely between the nose and the sinus cavities, gently washing away any inhaled bacteria, dust, or pollutants. Thus, anything that blocks these sinus passages will cause a problem; the obstruction of the normal flow of mucus out of the sinus will result in an area ripe for bacterial multiplication.

Signs of sinusitis in birds include sneezing, nasal discharge, runny eyes, and possible swelling around the eyes or face. Sinusitis is a serious condition, in that once firmly established it is extremely difficult to treat or to cure bacterial infections in this location.

Several nutritional deficiencies have been implicated in predisposing birds to this condition. In vitamin A deficiency, excessive squamous growth can result in obstruction of the narrow passages between the sinuses with thickened mucus or keratin. Once blocked, the sinus can become filled with mucus, providing a breeding ground for bacteria. Vitamin C has been shown to have beneficial effects on sinusitis in human studies. In humans, vitamin C acts as an

antihistamine, reducing the effects of allergies in sinusitis. It also has some function in stimulating the immune system. Allergies have not been confirmed in birds, although they are suspected, particularly in blue and gold macaws. Whether or not histamine plays a role in the symptoms of allergies in birds is also not known. Still, because vitamin C is often not provided in seed diets, the addition of foods high in vitamin C content may have beneficial effects. Ensuring adequate dietary zinc has also been recommended for humans with sinusitis, due to its known beneficial effects in stimulating the immune system, and for its role in the transportation of vitamin A from the liver so that it can be used in the rest of the body. This element may also have these same beneficial effects in avian species for the same reasons.

A nondietary item that can help to prevent sinusitis and that should be addressed is humidity levels.

Chronic sinusitis can result in permanent beak deformity.

Increased environmental humidity keeps the mucous membranes moist and prevents the drying out of mucus. A humidifier in the winter is an extremely useful preventive measure, provided the humidifier is kept clean so that the water within it does not become a breeding ground for bacteria.

Hypovitaminosis E

Vitamin E deficiency has been recognized to have several serious effects in poultry, and similar conditions have been reported in pet birds. It is required for reproduction, normal embryonal development, and the maintenance of a healthy immune system. It is also extremely important as an antioxidant within the body, preventing functional and/or physical damage to cell membranes.

Vitamin E deficiency results in liver necrosis (destruction), increased destruction of the red

Drooping wings, weakness, and uncoordination may be due to vitamin E deficiency, (although heavy metal toxicity must also be ruled out).

blood cells, reproductive failure, encephalomalacia, exudative diathesis, myodystrophy, and weakness. Reproductive failure is characterized by infertility in males and reduced egg hatchability. Encephalo-malacia is characterized by ataxia, incoordination, abnormal head movements, and a reluctance to walk. Lesions are found within the cerebellum of the brain, which is often soft, swollen, and hemorrhagic. Exudative diathesis describes a condition in which there is a buildup of fluid under the skin of the chest and abdomen. The buildup of fluid is a result of the increased permeability of capillary walls caused by damage by free radicals, the chemical substances vitamin E normally neutralizes. Myodystrophy, or muscular dystrophy, results in light-colored streaks in muscle tissue that can be seen with the naked eye. These light-colored streaks are actually sites of muscle cell degeneration or faulty formation, and they can also occur in the heart muscle, resulting in heart failure. "Cockatiel paralysis syndrome" describes a form of paralysis seen in cockatiels that is responsive to vitamin E-selenium injections.

Because vitamin E is a fat-soluble vitamin, depletion of body stores occurs fairly slowly. Diets high in polyunsaturated fats or diets that contain rancid fat promote vitamin E deficiency. Cod-liver oil, often used by aviculturists as a vitamin A and D supplement, is high in polyunsaturated fats and low in vitamin E.

Some of the signs of vitamin E deficiency may be reversed with supplementation, although encephalomalacia may not respond to therapy.

Diarrhea

There is a common misconception that fruits and vegetables cause diarrhea in pet birds. This is simply not true. It is true that fruits and vegetables add more moisture to the stool, but in most cases, what owners are observing is polyuria, not diarrhea. Polyuria means increased urine, and it is natural that ingesting a wetter food will cause an increase in urine production, just as drinking more water will increase our urine production. You can tell the difference between polyuria and diarrhea quite easily. In polyuria, the fecal portion of the stool is still formed; what you see is a large wet puddle, with a wormlike piece of fecal matter in the middle of it. In diarrhea, the fecal part of the stool is not formed, and appears more as a green or brown blob of yogurtlike consistency.

Diarrhea is in fact fairly rare in pet birds. When it does occur, it may indicate a bacterial or a viral infection, or a problem of malabsorption, such as in pancreatic or liver disease, or in certain protozoal infections, as will be discussed further along in this chapter.

If you suspect your bird does have diarrhea, take the bird and the papers from the cage to your avian veterinarian. If your veterinarian agrees with your assessment of the droppings, she or he will likely wish to run some diagnostic tests on your bird, or on a fresh stool sample.

Constipation

Constipation is seen even less frequently than diarrhea in pet bird practice, though it is often reported by owners. What most owners are actually observing is a decrease in the number of droppings the bird is producing. This is most often caused by a decrease in food consumption by the bird rather than by actual constipation.

Constipation can be caused by bowel obstruction due to foreign bodies the bird has ingested, or by egg binding obstructing the cloaca of the bird.

In either case, as with diarrhea, take the papers as well as your pet with you to show your avian veterinarian so that your observations can be properly assessed or verified.

Goiter

Goiter refers to hyperplasia (excess growth) of the thyroid gland caused by iodine deficiency. It is a common condition in budgerigars, although it has been seen in other species as well.

Classic signs of hypothyroidism in a budgerigar.

The characteristic signs of goiter in budgerigars include increased swallowing motions, crop emptying disorders, regurgitation, lethargy, anemia, cardiovascular changes, and tail-bobbing dyspnea. Tail-bobbing dyspnea refers to signs of labored respiration where the bird moves its entire tail up and down in order to increase the "bellows" action of its air sacs to move more air through the lungs. Because of its location at the thoracic inlet, it has long been believed that as the thyroid gland increases in size it puts pressure on the trachea and interferes with the outflow tract of the crop, leading to some of the characteristic signs this condition causes. However, Greg Harrison (author of *Clinical Avian Medicine and Surgery*) believes that it is excess fluid secretion in the crop and trachea that causes these clinical signs rather than actual obstruction by the enlarged thyroid gland.

Treatment consists of iodine supplementation, which can be accomplished by the use of Lugol's iodine in the drinking water, iodized seed, or mineral supplements that contain iodine.

Hypothyroidism

Hypothyroidism can occur with or without obvious signs of goiter. Hypothyroidism refers to a failure to produce adequate amounts of thyroid hormone, and is most often caused by iodine deficiency.

Clinical signs of deficiency include lethargy, a fluffed appearance, heat-seeking behavior, a reduced metabolic rate, increased fat deposition, and a change in feather structure. Lipomas, which are benign fat tumors, are common in hypothyroid birds, and will often regress dramatically once the hypothyroidism is treated. Another characteristic sign of hypothyroidism in budgies is the development of excessively long down feathers. These first appear under the wings, but will eventually occur all over the body. I have seen severe cases where the bird looked like some sort of animated dust bunny from under the bed! Other abnormalities such as decreased fertility, hypercholesteremia, and an increased susceptibility to infection are also suspected to be caused by hypothyroidism.

Iodine supplementation may be sufficient to reverse hypothyroidism if iodine deficiency is the cause, but in some cases thyroid supplementation is required. Consult your avian veterinarian regarding the treatment regimen your bird requires.

Obesity

Obesity is a very common problem in pet birds, particularly those on seed diets. As discussed in the chapter on the building blocks of nutrition, a bird will eat to exceed its energy requirements if the protein level of the diet is too low. The fact that seeds are deficient in adequate protein causes the bird to eat in amounts exceeding its normal energy requirements. The combination of an excessive intake of carbohydrates and fats, coupled with insufficient exercise, results in obesity, although it may also be secondary to diabetes mellitus, malnutrition, or hypothyroidism. Lipomas and fatty liver disease are common sequelae to obesity. Regardless of the initiating cause, there is no doubt that diet modification and an increase in activity level is beneficial in reducing excess body fat.

In most cases, simply converting from a seed diet to a better plane of nutrition will eliminate obesity. In other cases, increasing activity levels will also help. If the changes in diet discussed in this book do not result in a decrease in obesity in your bird, consult with your avian practitioner regarding the possibility of some other underlying cause of your bird's weight problem.

Fatty Liver Syndrome

Fatty liver syndrome is extremely common in pet birds. Various causes for the condition have been suggested, but there is no doubt that diet plays a major role in the course of this disease. Any bird on a seed-only diet is likely to be afflicted with this condition to a greater or lesser degree, whether it is readily apparent to the owner or not.

Fatty liver in a cockatiel.

Fatty liver is characterized by a fatty infiltration of the liver tissue. The most common concurrent signs of fatty liver disease include obesity, pale chest musculature, and a decrease in clotting ability. The beak and nails are often overgrown, and often have red-brown to black spots of hemorrhage in them.

The exact cause of fatty liver in psittacines is unclear, but it is due to a disruption of normal fat metabolism. The liver converts free fatty acids to triglycerides, which are then secreted into the circulation as lipoproteins. Normally there is an active shuttle of fatty substances between the liver and the fat tissue of the body. The synthesis of the protein part of the lipoprotein occurs only in the liver and is the rate-limiting step in the process. It is believed that in avian fatty liver disease the synthesis of triglycerides outstrips the liver's ability to produce lipoproteins that can be secreted into the plasma. This has been determined because often the large amounts of lipid that accumulate in the liver are synthesized in the liver. Glucagon, secreted by the pancreas, may also be involved, in that it is known that it limits or may even decrease the synthesis of the protein portion of lipoproteins. The accumulation of fat in the liver is accompanied by several biochemical processes, which include changes in the activities of enzymes, first by increases due to increased metabolic activi-

ty, followed by degeneration of the liver due to an increase in cellular lipid accumulation. Eventually the accumulation of lipid within the cells disrupts normal cellular activity and the cell dies. Cellular destruction leads to fibrosis, eventually destroying the normal structure of the liver.

There are several recognized causes of fatty liver. In psittacines, the most common causes are a diet high in fat or cholesterol; a diet too high in carbohydrates and too low in protein; and deficient transport of fat from the liver due to dietary deficiencies in choline, inositol, pyridoxine, pantothenic acid, protein, or essential fatty acids. Other causes include: excess administration of certain vitamins such as thiamine or biotin (although a similar condition in chickens called "Fatty Liver and Kidney Syndrome" is caused by biotin deficiency); increased mobilization of fat from adipose tissue caused by stress, starvation, insulin deficiency, hypoglycemia, or hormonal imbalance; and liver damage due to chemical or bacterial toxins, vitamin E deficiency, or anoxia (a lack of oxygen) caused by chronic anemia.

As mentioned above, lipoprotein synthesis is the rate-limiting step in fat metabolism in the liver. Substances that improve lipoprotein synthesis are called lipotropes. Choline is the most effective lipotrope, although methionine can replace choline to some extent. Inositol is also present in phospholipids and is effective in certain types of fatty liver. Although these lipotropic agents have recently fallen out of favor in dog and cat medicine for various reasons, they may still be of importance in the treatment of this condition in avian medicine, because we know avian diets are often deficient in choline and methionine.

An overall improvement in the quality of the diet will reduce excess fat and carbohydrates, increase protein, and supply all of the nutritional elements currently implicated in the cause of this disease.

Giardiasis

Giardiasis is an intestinal infection caused by the protozoal organism Giardia. Birds become contaminated by ingesting contaminated feces, or food or water that has been contaminated with feces, from an infected animal. The condition is considered very common in cockatiels and budgerigars in California. The cysts of giardia are resistant to chlorine, so it is important to boil water to kill the cysts. Fruits and vegetables that are grown in this area should also be washed well to eliminate any fecal contamination that may have occurred from wild animal vectors of the disease before the food was harvested. Rats and other vector hosts may also be sources of the disease in aviaries and should be eliminated.

Although the infection is not one of purely nutritional origin, it is men-tioned here because of the effects it has on digestion and the digestive system. Chronic diarrhea, weight loss, and death can occur as a result of infection. A foamy, foul-smelling, yellow-brown diarrhea may be produced, and feather problems may occur because the condition blocks the absorption of the fat-soluble vitamins. Dr. Alan Fudge, an avian veterinarian in California, believes that giardiasis is the most common cause of feather picking in cockatiels in California, especially if these birds are also showing signs of loose, voluminous stools. It has been implicated as one of the causes of feather picking in other species as well.

An accurate diagnosis can be difficult, because the organism is only shed intermittently in the stool and is difficult to identify even microscopically.

Your avian veterinarian can prescribe a treatment, but relapses are common and repeated treatment may be necessary.

Trichomoniasis

Trichomoniasis is caused by a protozoal organism called Trichomonas gallinae. It is often seen in pigeons, finches, canaries, and budgerigars, and occasionally occurs in parrots. In pigeons, the disease is often transmitted from adult birds to their babies by feeding, via the crop milk the adult pigeon produces. Birds can also become infected by drinking or eating food that has become contaminated by an infected bird. Wild pigeons can infect an aviary by passing stools into the aviary, illustrating another reason why it is important to protect outside aviaries from wild birds.

The disease can produce two kinds of lesions. In the "wet canker" form, the lesions seen are raw ulcerations in the mouth, esophagus, and oropharynx. If the lesions are severe, raspy, labored breathing may occur. In the "dry canker" form, the lesions are filled with caseous (cheeselike) pus. In young birds the disease is often fatal. In adult birds, the disease is usually chronic, with weight loss and weakness being the most common clinical signs, although vomiting and diarrhea may also be seen. The condition can also produce a serious, often fatal, infection in baby parrots.

The diagnosis is made by using a microscope to find the protozoal organisms in a sample from the sick bird. The organism is usually fairly easy to demonstrate in pigeons and budgerigars, but can be very difficult to diagnose in parrots.

Stress conditions such as overcrowding and poor hygiene contribute to outbreaks of the disease. The organism cannot survive for long outside of the host; therefore, maintaining a clean environment is important in disease control. Your avian veterinarian can prescribe the correct drug to treat the condition. Prompt treatment is vital to prevent fatalities in baby birds. As with giardiasis, total elimination of the organism is difficult, and repeated treatments may be necessary.

Other Protozoal Infections

Other protozoal intestinal infections that can occur in pet birds include histomoniasis, toxoplasmosis, hexamitiasis, and coccidiosis. These protozoal conditions are fairly rare in pet birds, so they will not be discussed further, other than to say that if diarrhea occurs in your pet bird your veterinarian will likely want to examine a fresh fecal sample in order to rule out a parasitic cause of the diarrhea.

Starvation

Starvation is the ultimate nutritional deficiency, and can occur from a variety of causes. Failing to provide food is the most obvious cause, and is a more common occurrence than one would like to believe. Because seeds have husks, the bird will husk the seed and leave the husk in the food dish. An unobservant owner can mistake a dish full of empty husks as a dish that still contains food.

Other causes also exist. A more dominant cage mate may prevent a weaker individual from having access to the food dish. An ill bird, or a bird with throat lesions caused by trauma or candidiasis, may refuse to eat. Beak deformity caused by an overgrown beak, or beak distortion caused by scaly face and leg mite, may also interfere with a bird's ability to eat.

Psychological disturbances, such as excessive regurgitation may also occur. I once had a budgerigar patient that would go through a dessert bowl of seed a day, first eating it, then regurgitating it to his mirror, leaving piles of seed below it. In spite of this massive seed consumption, the bird was wasting away, because he didn't digest most of what he consumed.

The saddest cause of starvation occurs when an owner is not observant when trying to convert a bird from a seed diet to a better diet. As described in the chapter Changing the Diet, be sure to monitor the amount of droppings the bird is producing. For example, as stated, a normal budgerigar produces between 18 to 24 droppings in a 24-hour period. If the normal number of droppings your bird produces decreases by more than 20 percent, or if all the droppings are smaller than normal and contain less fecal material, there may be a problem and you should have your bird examined to check for excessive weight loss.

Chapter 8
Diet-related Toxins

Toxins in the Environment

Birds in the wild spend a great deal of their time exploring their environment with their beak—manipulating, chewing, tasting, and nibbling. A bird who flies around freely in your home will engage in similar activities, often without your knowledge. Many an owner has turned around to discover that his or her unusually quiet pet is pruning a plant, remodeling some furniture, or dismantling a favorite pair of earrings. Any of these items contain potentially harmful substances, including poisonous plant alkaloids, wood preservatives, and heavy metals such as lead or zinc.

A parrot flying free in your home can get into anything when your back is turned.

Toxins in Plants

It is fairly certain that if your bird has access to plants in its environment it will sample the plant at one point or another. Although few plant toxicity studies have been conducted with pet birds, it is generally considered that any plant that has been shown to have harmful effects in man, poultry, or other animals should also be considered to have potentially harmful effects in pet birds as well. Note that I said "potentially harmful"; a very good article on poisonous plants by avian veterinarian Cathy Johnson-Delaney in the March 1990 issue of Bird Talk was followed by a rebuttal letter by an aviculturist claiming that his birds had eaten several of the plants on the toxic list and had suffered no ill effects. Some other anecdotal reports have also claimed that birds have been seen eating plants considered toxic without any signs of toxicity. Nonetheless, signs of toxicity may not be immediately apparent, or may be more subtle and long-term. Unless actual plant toxicity studies have been carried out for that species of plant with your species of bird, it is

best to avoid those plants known to be toxic in other animals, and to stick with those plants that are known to be safe.

Plant toxicity can occur in a number of ways. Some plants are immediately toxic, in that they cause illness or death immediately upon ingestion. Others cause allergies, skin inflammation, or temporary irritation to the mucous membranes of the mouth or throat. Still others can cause changes in cells, which can lead to cancer or deformities in the offspring of the bird. Table 6, page 108, lists plants that are considered to be safe, whereas Table 7, page 108, lists those plants currently considered to be toxic. Even if the plant may be considered safe, beware of the buildup of fertilizer around the edges of the planter; many birds have been known to nibble on this substance with serious consequences. Make a point of cleaning off this buildup regularly, and be cautious in your use of fertilizers in the plants your bird has access to.

Toxins in Wood

Chewing wood is a common pastime for birds in the wild, and it can also have a healthy psychological effect on birds in captivity as well. However, chewing certain wood items may have toxic effects. Certain preservatives, stains, or varnishes are potentially toxic. Older homes may have lead-based paints on the walls or woodwork; this can be a source of serious toxicity for pet birds. Even in their natural state, certain woods contain toxic substances; for example, horse chestnut and oak wood are not considered safe. Apple, maple, ash, elm, magnolia, and any citrus wood are examples of woods that are considered safe, and can be used to furnish perches, or to make chew toys.

Make sure the house-plants your bird has access to are safe.

Common potentially poisonous house plants. Top right: rhododendron; bottom left: calidium; bottom right, dieffenbachia.

Toxins in Metal

Lead and zinc toxicosis from ingesting items containing these substances is extremely common, and is often missed by pet bird owners. Lead solder, costume jewelry, zipper teeth, Tiffany lamps, and curtain weights are just a few examples of sources of heavy metal toxicity I have seen over the years. Unless treated promptly, heavy metal intoxication will result in death, or at best, in permanent nervous system damage. If you know your bird has eaten something metal, or if your bird is showing any neurological signs, such as weakness, lack of balance, stupor, tremors, or seizures, it should be seen by your avian veterinarian immediately.

Toxins in the Cage

Birds confined to their cages may also be exposed to possible environmental toxins. Poisonous plants, woodwork, or walls may still be reached through cage bars if an owner is not observant in cage placement. Hazards can also exist inside the cage. Loose bits of solder or zinc coating from the cage bars can be ingested inadvertently as the bird "walks" around the cage bars; it is important to scrub new cages down thoroughly to remove any loose bits of solder or zinc coating that may remain from the construction process. New cages made from galvanized wire have often been implicated in "new cage disease," a term used to refer to zinc toxicosis originating from this source. Toys that are inappropriate for your bird are often sources of toxicity; the lead-weighted penguins that are popular for budgerigars can be dismantled by larger parrots, which then eat the lead weight inside them. Clangors inside bells, loose screws, and bits of wire can also be eaten, as can chunks of plastic that can obstruct the digestive tract. The cage environment should be inspected as thoroughly as the rest of the house to eliminate potential sources of environmental toxicity for your bird.

Toxins in Food

One of the questions I am asked frequently by my clients when a bird dies suddenly is, "Do you think there was something wrong with the food?" What they are actually asking is if the food was in some way poisonous. My answer frequently is, "Yes, there was something wrong with the food, but not what you think."

From all our previous discussions it should be evident to you that there are many ways in which nutrition influences disease that has nothing to do with toxic substances in the feed. Nonetheless, no discussion of diet would be complete without addressing some of the more important dietary toxicities of which you should be aware.

Bacterial Contamination

As addressed in the chapter Diet and Disease, bacteria

contamination of food is a frequent occurrence and is an important potential source of pathogenic bacteria for our pet birds. Following the advice given in The Importance of Good Hygiene section, page 79, will reduce your contribution to the problem, but what if the food is already contaminated before you receive it? Concerns regarding the bacterial contamination of seed caused quite an uproar a few years ago, but in fact any foodstuff can be contaminated if not processed correctly. For this reason it is important to choose high-quality products produced by reputable manufacturers that apply stringent quality control measures. If you have any doubts concerning the quality of the food, take a sample with you to your veterinarian and have it assessed. Some diagnostic procedures, such as a bacterial culture and sensitivity test, may be needed in order to properly analyze the food.

Molds and Fungi

Improperly stored seeds and grains may become contaminated with fungi and molds. Seeds and grains stored under conditions of high humidity, poor ventilation, and warm temperatures favor the growth of molds and fungi. Molds and fungi can produce toxic substances called mycotoxins. There are various types of mycotoxins that can be produced, and each has different toxic effects in the body. These toxins can remain in the food long after the fungus that produced them has died, and some remain toxic even after the food has been cooked.

Aflatoxicosis is a severe, often fatal, toxic syndrome caused by the ingestion of the mycotoxin produced by the fungus Aspergillus flavis. Aflatoxin causes a severe gastroenteritis and also destroys the tissue of the liver and kidney. Even in small amounts, this toxin can act as a potent cancer-causing agent. Peanuts are often contaminated with aflatoxin. Good quality commercial peanut butter is monitored for this toxin, but freshly ground peanut butter in bulk or health food stores usually is not, and studies have shown that it is often contaminated. For this reason it is advisable not to use anything but good quality commercial peanut butter for your pet birds to avoid this potential source of toxicity.

Ergot is a type of fungal toxin frequently found on moldy millet or canary seed. It is produced by a fungus called Claviceps purpurea. Ergot constricts blood vessels, leading to dry gangrene of the extremities. The toes, feet, and legs of birds can become black and fall off; an entire limb can be lost due to this serious fungal toxin. Vomiting, staggering, and sometimes death can also occur.

Always carefully examine any food you offer your pet bird. If there is any sign of mold, or if the food has a moldy odor, it should never be offered to your pet bird.

Avocados

Although some owners may report that their birds can eat guacamole without ill effects, a potential source of toxicosis has been recognized that is associated with several species of avocado. The toxin causes congestion in the lungs, subcutaneous edema (fluid accumulation beneath the skin), and fluid accumulation in the heart sac. Depressed appetite, labored breathing, and a fluffed, listless appearance may be seen, although in some cases, death occurs before the owner is even aware of any clinical signs.

For this reason avocados should not be fed to pet birds, particularly because there are many other good food sources available that do not carry this potential for toxicity.

Parsley

Parsley-induced photosensitivity has been reported in ostriches and ducks fed large quantities of parsley. Conjunctivitis (inflamed eye membranes), reddened eyelids, reddened skin, and scabs were seen in these birds, but only when they were exposed to unfiltered sunlight.

This report, and ones similar to it in other species, has led to rumors that parsley is toxic in pet birds. In fact, there is no evidence to suggest that the occasional ingestion of a sprig or two of parsley is harmful in any way to pet birds. Parsley is a good source of vitamins and is often favored by smaller species, such as canaries and finches, so there is no reason not to feed it in moderate amounts.

Goitrogens

Goitrogens are substances that are known to have a detrimental effect on the thyroid gland, promoting the formation of goiter. Several different types of goitrogenic substances exist in plants, and they were described in the section on iodine (see page 32).

Several dietary items are known to have goitrogenic activity, including rapeseed, cabbage, brussels sprouts, rutabagas, cauliflower, turnips, and peanuts. Because heat destroys goitrogens, these substances are generally considered harmful only if large quantities are eaten raw. Rapeseed is commonly found in pet bird seed mixes, especially in canary, finch, and budgerigar diets. The goitrogenic activity of rapeseed depends both on the amount of rapeseed ingested and on the species of bird ingesting it. For example, quail are more sensitive to its effects than turkeys.

Eliminating these food substances from the diet is unwarranted, because these foods contain many other nutritionally valuable components. As we have discussed throughout the book, balance and moderation are the keys to avoiding the harm that any dietary excess may cause.

Salt Toxicity

As discussed, sodium and chloride are essential minerals and play a key role in regulating fluid balance as well as a host of other functions in the body. A regular seed diet is more likely to be deficient in salt than cause salt toxicity, however, excessive salt intake can occur, particularly in pet birds that share their owner's meals and snacks. It is also important to note that water deprivation can promote salt toxicity; if water is freely available it will take high levels of salt to cause salt toxicity, however, if water is restricted, lower levels of salt can have toxic effects.

It is the sodium ion of salt that is believed to cause the toxic effects by building up in the cerebral spinal fluid of the brain, causing damage. Signs of toxicity in poultry include respiratory distress, wet feces, fluid from the beak, and paralysis of the limbs. If water is available, water intake is increased and food intake is decreased. High salt intake also raises blood pressure. Prolonged high blood pressure has the same detrimental effects in other species as it has in man, increasing the risk of heart disease and stroke.

Canned vegetables are high in salt and should be rinsed before use. In fact, many canned foods are high in salt content, as are pickled foods, snack foods, and some crackers. I once had a case where a blue and gold macaw shared a bag of potato chips with his owner in front of the television one night as they watched a movie. The next day the bird was dead due to salt toxicosis.

The occasional grain of salt is not harmful, provided your bird always has access to plenty of fresh water. However, it is important to realize that 10 or 20 grains of salt in a budgerigar would be the equivalent of a teaspoon or more of salt for us. For this reason, it is important to be cautious in regulating your bird's salt intake.

Pesticides and Herbicides

As we all know, various herbicides and pesticides are used by farmers in an effort to improve the quality of food as well as to increase yields. In most cases, the levels of these substances on foods by the time of harvest are minimal, and they are not much of a concern for us. However, these substances may still be present in sufficient quantities to have detrimental effects. For this reason it is always wise to wash all fruits and vegetables well, and to do the same with any fresh wood you may offer to chew, although it is best to offer wood that has not been exposed to these chemicals at all.

TABLE 6
Plants Considered Safe

Acacia	Dogwood	Nasturitum
African violet	Donkey tail	Norfolk Island pine
Aloe plant	Dracaena	Palms
Baby's tears	Dragon tree	Petunia
Bamboo	Ferns	Pittosporum
Begonia	Figs	Prayer plant
Bougainvillea	Gardenia	Rubber tree
Chickweed	Grape ivy	Schefflera
Christmas cactus	Hens and chickens	Sensitive plant
Coffee tree	Jade plant	Spider plant
Coleus	Kalanchoe	Swedish ivy
Corn plant	Magnolia	Thistle
Crab apple	Marigolds	Wandering Jew
Dandelion	Monkey plant	White clover
		Zebra plant

TABLE 7
Plants Considered Potentially Toxic

Avocado	Foxglove	Oleander
Azalea	Heliotrope	Periwinkle
Baneberry	Holly	Philodendrons
Bean plants	Honeysuckle	Pigweed
Bird of Paradise	Hydrangea	Poison ivy and oak
Bleeding Heart	Ivy	Pokeweed
Boxwood	Jasmine	Privet
Bracken fern	Jerusalem cherry	Purple sesbane
Buckthorn	Jimsonweed	Rain tree
Bulb flowers (amaryllis, iris,	Lantana	Red maple
daffodil, narcissus, hyacinth)	Larkspur	Rhubarb leaves
Burdock	Lily	Rhododendrons
Buttercup	Locusts	Sandbox tree
Coffee plants	Lupine	Skunk cabbage
Cowslip	May apple	Sorrel
Crown vetch	Milkweed	Snowdrop
Daphne	Mistletoe	Spurges
Dieffenbachia	Mock orange	Sweet Pea
Elderberry	Monkshood	Tobacco
Eucalyptus	Morning Glory	Vetch
Euonymus	Mountain Laurel	Wattle
Flame tree	Nettles	White cedar
Felt plant	Nightshade	Yews
Firethorn	Oak	

Chapter 9
Diet As It Relates to Specific Breeds

One thing that has become increasingly clear over the last few years in avian medicine is that there is no such thing as a generic parrot. Each species has its own unique characteristics, not only in personality and behavior, but also in more fundamental ways, such as variations in the way each metabolizes different drugs. It is no wonder, then, that we are beginning to discover that dietary needs are just as varied, with some species being more prone to certain deficiencies than others.

Many of these species' particular requirements are not known, or are only conjectured from the observations of various aviculturists and veterinarians. This chapter will attempt to draw these various observations together in one section. This chapter is not meant to be a definitive statement on these various species' needs, but rather to be a summary of various observations to be used as a starting point for proper scientific research or as a validation of some things you may have observed among your own birds.

Seed-only diets can result in a short life span and poor reproductive performance in finches.

Finches

Although finches are considered seed eaters, their diet in the wild varies widely depending on seasonal availability. Mature edible seeds are only available during one part of the season; at other times young sprouts and insects form the main basis of the diet. It is no wonder then that the seed-only diet we tend to offer these birds in captivity results in short life spans and poor reproductive performance.

Attempts to raise finches solely on pelleted rations has resulted in disappointment, causing finch owners to avoid pelleted rations altogether. This is not necessary, because we do know that feeding at least some pelleted rations is bound to provide a better quality diet than can seeds alone. Dr. David Henzler, author of *Healthy Diet, Healthy Bird*, suggests that the reason baby finches fail to thrive on pelleted rations is likely due to inadequate protein levels in the diet. He suggests adding one part of Zupreem Primate Dry monkey biscuit to one part moistened pellets or crumbles, and blenderizing it so that the consistency resembles a graham-cracker pie crust. This can be offered in a ratio of 1 teaspoon per pair of finches to 2 teaspoons of quality finch mix that includes 1/4 teaspoon added canary grass seed. He also suggests that a small amount of powdered vitamin/mineral mix be added to this, but I do not advocate this practice, because most pellets contain adequate vitamins and minerals already.

Aside from seeds, crumbles, sprouted seeds, vegetables, and fruit, live insects should also be offered, with the quantity increased during the breeding season. Insects are a good source of animal protein, although feeding too many can be fattening. The amount of insects

A bird with Canary Balding Syndrome.

to offer depends on the size of the finch, and the size of the insects; for example, one to two mealworms a day is plenty for most birds, with that amount being increased to four or five mealworms when there are babies in the nest. Alternatively, egg food can also provide a good protein source. Remember that egg yolk is high in cholesterol, so that one should not provide egg food daily in the nonbreeding season.

Canaries

Just as with finches, there are concerns that the pelleted formulations currently available do not meet all of a canary's needs for growth and reproduction. Generally, the recommendations made for finches can also be applied to canaries, especially the recommendation for providing animal protein in the diet. Dark, leafy green vegetables such as endive and escarole, are especially good vegetable choices because they are often well accepted by canaries and finches and are high in nutritive value.

Diet plays an important role in the expression of the so-called "red factor" in canaries. Red-factor canaries are those birds that have a red-orange genetic background as a result of an original hybridization with the Venezuelan black-hooded red siskin. This red factor is influenced by diet, in that feeding certain foods brings out the red color in the feathers of these birds. The degree to which the red-orange pigmentation is exhibited is as much a function of the bird's genetic background as it is of the use of coloring agents or certain foods. In other words, even with the same foods or coloring agents, a bird with a good red-orange genetic background will show better red-orange coloration than a bird of poorer genetic background, thus accounting for color differences in birds fed the same diet.

Canaries are also prone to a condition referred to as Canary Balding Syndrome. In this condition, feathers are lost over the back of the neck first, then from the head and the rest of the body. The feathers are not replaced, and the bird can become quite bald over time. This condition occurs in both male and female canaries, and in several species of finches. The cause of the condition is not known, but it is known to respond to testosterone supplementation. I suspect that the cause of this condition is nutritional, and likely results because of a vitamin, mineral, or amino acid deficiency that interferes with the normal production of the testosterone hormone.

Budgerigars

Goiter, hypothyroidism, obesity, and fatty liver syndrome are all commonly recognized nutritional diseases in budgerigars. Of all the pet bird species, mature budgerigars are among the most difficult birds to convert from a seed diet, yet they are one of the species most likely to benefit from a better level of nutrition. They are extremely stubborn, and mixing pellets with seed is often unsuccessful, because they insist on eating around them. In budgies, the preferred method of conversion is to withhold the regular seed mix until noon, and offer the new foods first thing in the day when the bird is hungriest. One of

Budgerigars are prone to goiter, hypothyroidism, obesity and fatty liver syndrome.

the easier ways to first introduce pelleted feeds is by offering a product like Lafeber's Avi-Cakes, where seeds and pelleted diets have been mixed together in a biscuit-type form. Lafeber's Nutri-Berries provide a combination of hulled seed, peanut hearts, vitamins, minerals, carbohydrates, and essential amino acids from whole eggs presented in a berrylike form. Even if your bird has refused other types of diet improvement, these foods are likely to be accepted and at least give you a start. Once the bird has accepted these into its diet, you can eventually switch to pellets.

Groups of four or more budgies are more likely to sample a new food source, so conversion in groups of this size housed together appears to be less difficult. It should be noted, however, that in a group of two or more birds, the females will have the greatest tendency towards obesity. Female budgerigars tend to be more dominant than male birds, and one aspect of establishing dominance lies in "lording it" over the food dish, thus increasing their food intake over normal maintenance levels.

Cockatiels

The conditions of obesity and of fatty liver syndrome are also common in cockatiels. The appearance of excessively yellow feathers in Lutino cockatiels can indicate liver disease, possibly caused by an infectious agent, fatty liver syndrome, or a deficiency of essential amino acids, choline, or riboflavin. Many owners are pleased with the bright yellow color of the feathers in these birds, but it is important to be aware that this color is unhealthy; healthy Lutino cockatiels are more white than bright yellow in coloration.

Feather picking is a common problem in cockatiels. Although the condition is often psychological, the intestinal infection giardiasis should also be considered. Deficiency of the essential amino acid arginine may also play a role.

Cockatiel paralysis describes a condition in which cockatiels show sudden signs of weakness or paralysis, especially of the wings and legs. This condition appears to be vitamin E/selenium responsive. It is thought that giardiasis may also be responsible for this condition by causing a malabsorption of vitamins, or that the presence of rancid fat in the diet may destroy vitamin E.

Chronic egg laying cockatiels are almost always hypocalcemic, and

Chronic egg-laying cockatiels are usually hypocalcemic.

can suffer from osteomalacia, egg binding, and nutritional secondary hyperparathyroidism.

Some cockatiels that are extremely pair-bonded with their owners may pine and refuse to eat when separated from them.

As with budgerigars, switching from a seed-only diet to pelleted rations will likely aid in preventing these conditions.

Lovebirds

Lovebirds is a name regarded as a misnomer among avian veterinarians, because lovebirds are among one of the more aggressive species. It is not unusual for lovebirds to draw blood or inflict serious injuries on a cage mate. For this reason, it is better to provide more food and water dishes, so that at least this aspect of cohabitation does not serve as a source of conflict between the birds.

Giardiasis is being recognized with increasing frequency in lovebirds, particularly in birds in California. In lovebirds the symptoms are general illness, diarrhea, and feather picking.

Egg yolk peritonitis (inflammation of the abdomen caused by the abnormal release of egg yolks into the abdomen instead of down the oviduct) and egg binding are common in lovebirds and are often caused by calcium deficiency.

Pelleted rations will help improve the general health of this species. In addition, a daily supply of fresh leafy greens, carrot sticks, or broccoli flowerets attached to the side of the cage will give this species something on which to release their aggressive tendencies, and may help to promote a better sense of psychological well-being.

Conures

Conures appear to be more likely to develop abnormal bleeding episodes than other species. For this reason, the addition of dietary sources rich in vitamin K, such as turnip greens and kale, are highly recommended for conures, as are the addition of sources rich in calcium, such as cheese, broccoli, and oyster shell.

Conures are also recognized as a species that commonly feather pick. The most common cause in this species appears to be

Conures are prone to Conure Bleeding Syndrome.

114

behavioral, but there may be an unrecognized dietary component, such as arginine, that may be involved. It may simply be that, like the African gray, these are intelligent, high-strung birds that require a more emotionally and psychologically rewarding environment than we generally provide in captivity in order to thrive.

Doves and Pigeons

There are close to three hundred species of pigeons and doves distributed worldwide, so naturally their dietary needs vary with each species. Basically, they can be divided into three groups: the seed-eating pigeons and doves of the Old and New Worlds; the fruit pigeons of Africa, Australia, Asia, and the East Indies; and the giant crowned pigeons of New Guinea and the surrounding area. The majority of pigeons and doves are primarily seed, grain, and fruit eaters, however, some species do eat insects, worms, grubs, and snails.

Pigeons and doves in captivity often suffer from calcium deficiency, because most people only offer them commercially available seed mixes. This is completely unnecessary, because there are many commercially available pigeon pellets on the market, and almost all of these birds accept this addition to the diet easily. Seeds should form no more than 50 percent of these birds' daily diet;

whole wheat bread, pigeon pellets, and finely-chopped greens, such as Swiss chard or kale, should also be offered, as well as mealworms or other live insects and fruit (depending on the bird species), and the addition of oyster shell or crumbled eggshells.

As mentioned briefly in the chapter on anatomy, both pigeon parents feed the chicks with "crop milk." As the birds incubate the eggs, the crop lining thickens, and when the babies hatch, this lining breaks off into cheesy curds that the adult birds regurgitate to the young. This crop milk is high in nutritive value, and is fed to the young for the first few weeks of life. At that time, half-digested seeds and berries are regurgitated from the crop until the time of weaning, usually three to four weeks after hatching. Naturally, crop milk is high in protein, so it is especially important to provide good quality protein in the diet during reproduction.

Lories and Lorikeets

Lories and lorikeets feed on a wide range of soft foods and insects in the wild, including nectar and pollen. In order to maintain these birds properly, let alone enjoy any success in breeding, we must mimic this natural diet as closely as possible. Fortunately, there are a number of nectar and pollen substitutes available commercially that help make this job easier. In addition to these food sources, a fruit salad of apples, pears, peaches, pineapples, strawberries, seedless grapes, carrots, and a shredded dark leafy green vegetable, such as kale or endive, should also be added. The third part of a balanced diet varies somewhat with the individual species; live insects and/or soft ripe fresh seeds such as millet, canary grass seed, oat groats, wheat, and buckwheat, can be added depending on the species of lory or lorikeet involved. This is an area where individual research on your species' diet in the wild is of great value in helping to formulate a balanced diet.

Because of the moist nature of the diet in this species, proper food hygiene and cage cleanliness are essential in order to avoid bacterial and yeast infections. These birds must also have continuous access to clean bath water, so that they can clean the sticky food from their plumage and beaks.

Mynahs

As with many fruit eaters, mynahs have a relatively short digestive tract. I have seen a mynah eat a cherry or blueberry, and pass red or blue droppings 15 minutes later! Their droppings are often moist and sloppy, and this species is often quite active, jumping from perch to perch, so that the cage often becomes soiled and must be cleaned regularly. This is particularly true of the perches, which tend to become caked with a thin layer of food debris and are often neglected in most people's cage-cleaning efforts.

Mynah birds are prone to the iron storage disease called hemochromatosis. Although the exact cause of this disease is not known (suggested causes are discussed in the Diet and Disease chapter), it is thought that a diet with a lower than average iron content may help to slow the disease. It should be noted, however, that birds on low-iron diets may still succumb, and birds on high-iron diets may not, so that the recommendations regarding a low-iron diet are debatable. Nonetheless, several commercial products that are suitable for mynahs contain dietary iron levels of below 150 mg/kg, for example, Marion's Zoological Scenic Low Iron Ration, and Science Diet Canine Maintenance dog kibble.

Red meat is high in iron content, therefore red meat and liver may not be the best choices as animal protein sources for this species. Cooked egg whites are low in iron and are a good source of animal protein. Boiled potatoes, yogurt, apples, bananas, grapes, pears, pineapples, plums, oranges, figs, and watermelons are other foods that are also low in iron content, although they should not be considered complete protein sources.

Folic acid and choline deficiency have been found to contribute to this disease in humans. For this reason, I suggest that ensuring that the diet contain adequate levels of these nutrients may be beneficial in susceptible species.

Toucans and Toucanets

Toucans and toucanets move about the jungle in small flocks, following the fruits and berries as they ripen. Small rodents, insects, lizards, and bird eggs also form an important part of their diet.

Like most of the fruit-eaters, these birds produce wet droppings that are ideal breeding grounds for pathogenic bacteria if strict hygiene practices are not followed.

Their diet should consist of a fruit salad of apples, cherries, pears, peaches, pineapple, figs, bananas, seedless grapes, berries, tomatoes, shredded carrots, Swiss chard, and kale, as well as bread, insects, eggs, "pinkie" mice, and soft-bill diet (described in the Recipes chapter, page 120). These species eat their food whole, so it is important to cut the food into chunks of an appropriate size for your species.

As with mynahs, toucans are also prone to hemochromatosis. The cause of the disease is also not known in this species, but experiments with iron-reduced diets are currently underway. Dietary suggestions are listed above in the section on mynahs.

Amazons

Amazons are particularly prone to vitamin A deficiency, sinusitis, calcium deficiency, and obesity. In most cases, it is the tendency of these birds to eat nothing but sunflower seeds or peanuts that causes these problems, resulting in a high-fat, low-nutritive value diet. These birds benefit dramatically from the dietary improvements discussed throughout this book, including good food sources of vitamin A and C, calcium, animal protein, pelleted rations, and four-food-group feeding.

Amazons are among those species that love to hold a food item in their foot in order to pry off tasty morsels. For this reason, carrot sticks, broccoli flowerets, green

Amazons are prone to hypovitaminosis A, sinusitis, calcium deficiency, and obesity.

beans, cheese sticks, and any foods that can be easily held in the foot are considered wonderful "play" foods for this species.

African Grays

African grays are particularly susceptible to hypocalcemia syndrome, hypovitaminosis A, sinusitis, and feather abnormalities. The appearance of red feathers in place of gray feathers is believed to be caused by a deficiency of the essential amino acid lysine. Feather picking is common in this species and is most often behavioral, although a deficiency in the essential amino acid arginine may be involved. An improvement in basic nutrition can go a long way in treating this condition, particularly if the play value of food is emphasized. African gray parrots are extremely intelligent and high strung, and really seem to suffer in an unstimulating environment. Making life interesting by improving the environment and by providing an active outlet for chewing and beak manipulation with interesting foods and food locations can go a long way to reducing the boredom that drives many of these birds to feather pick.

Cockatoos

Cockatoos are highly social animals, and many hand-raised babies would prefer to be surgically grafted to their owners than to have to be alone. Their strong emotional needs can be important in their diet selection; it is not unusual for cockatoos to pine for their owners and refuse to eat if they are deprived of companionship. Wild-caught cockatoos can be extremely stubborn when it comes to accepting new dietary items.

Cockatoos are very susceptible to psittacine beak and feather syndrome. Because this condition can often first appear as an overgrown beak and nails and a loss of powder down, some people may suspect that the bird simply suffers from a nutritional deficiency rather than a disease. For this reason, feather abnormalities in cockatoos

Rose-breasted cockatoos have an increased incidence of fatty tumors.

should always be seen by an avian veterinarian first before presuming the cause is purely nutritional.

Rose-breasted cockatoos have been reported to have an increased incidence of fatty tumors. The cause of the condition is unknown, but it is likely that an excess of dietary fat is involved, particularly in birds that ingest large amounts of sunflower seeds.

Macaws

Certain species of macaws have been noted to eat large quantities of palm nuts in the wild. These nuts are known to have a high level of fat, leading to suspicions that these species have a much higher fat requirement than other species of parrots, particularly if they are to breed successfully. Keep in mind, however, that this higher level of fat must also be accompanied by an adequate level of dietary protein in order for the fat to be metabolized properly.

Psittacine proventricular dilatation syndrome appears to be particularly common in young blue and gold and green-wing macaws. Hand-raised babies are susceptible to stress-bar formation in their juvenile plumage, although these feathers are replaced with normal feathers at the first molt. Hand-raised babies may also develop the habit of regurgitating for their owners, an action that may be misinterpreted as vomiting.

Hypervitaminosis D and stunting syndrome have both been recognized commonly in baby blue and gold macaws, and are related to poor hand-feeding diet formulations.

Certain species of macaws may have higher fat requirements than other bird species.

Conclusion

Although each species has its own particular needs, there is no doubt that a general improvement in the quality of the diet will go a long way in satisfying these needs. Although I have suggested that certain foods may be more beneficial than others for certain species, do not be tempted to oversupplement, particularly with increased amounts of food additive products available commercially. Overuse of these products can undoubtedly do more harm than good.

Chapter 10
Recipes

The recipes that follow are only a few examples of those currently used by aviculturists around the world. You should view them not as a definitive answer on how to feed your bird, but rather as examples of how you can apply the principles that I have discussed throughout the book. It is my hope that these examples will stimulate you to experiment on your own while providing you with useful guidelines.

Always remember three essential points regarding diet formulation. First, remember to provide food from all four food groups. Second, the greater the variety in the diet the more likely that any deficiency present will be compensated for. Third, make sure your bird is eating all the parts of the diet you are providing, or all of your efforts to provide a bal-anced feeding regimen will be wasted. If one ingredient is not accepted, try substituting one of similar nutritive value that is acceptable.

Soft Food Diet

This diet is a variation on the original soft food diet recommended by Dr. Raymond Kray. It is often used as a transitional diet when trying to convert birds from seeds to pellets, although it can be fed as most of the regular basic diet as well. This food does spoil quickly, so it is best to freeze individual portions and just thaw a portion as needed, being sure to remove the food and wash the food dishes in the cage twice daily. It will also cause a softer, lighter colored stool to be produced that will have a stronger odor. This is normal, and not a cause for alarm.

Ingredients:
Equal portions of:
- Whole kernel corn (fresh, frozen, or canned)
- Cooked brown or white rice
- Legumes (lentils, kidney beans, split peas, chick-peas, lima beans,

An example of the "soft food diet."

black-eyed peas, navy or pinto beans)
• Dry dog food or parrot pellets

Directions:

1. The amount of ingredients used depends on how much of the diet you choose to make up and store at one time, although you should not make up more than your bird can eat in a six-month period. A reasonable volume for one bird for a few months would be roughly 2 cans of corn, 2 cans of legumes, 2 cups of cooked rice, and a little under 2 cups of pellets. This is stored in yogurt tubs (about 2 cups [a 500 ml tub] hold roughly three days worth of food for an Amazon and can be kept refrigerated for that length of time), or in individual portion size plastic bags that can be frozen and thawed individually.

2. If using canned corn, be sure to rinse it thoroughly prior to use to decrease the levels of salt, because most canned corn is packed in salt water.

3. If using dried beans or peas, soak the legumes overnight, then rinse thoroughly in running water. Cover the legumes with fresh water, and boil for 8 to 10 minutes before use. Reserve the water drained from the beans. If canned legumes are used, rinse thoroughly prior to use to remove the excess salt. Canned legumes need not be cooked prior to use.

4. Cook the rice as you normally would (i.e. 1 portion rice to 2 portions water for approximately 20 minutes). Brown rice contains higher levels of thiamine, but white rice can be used. If using dried legumes, use the water reserved from the boiled beans to cook the rice in, because some of the vitamins leached from the legumes during the cooking process are contained in it. For some birds, flavoring the rice can enhance the acceptability of the diet. Onion powder, marjoram, chili powder, garlic, or a tablespoon of peanut butter or frozen orange juice concentrate have all been used to enhance the flavor, depending on the bird's preferences. (Be sure to test which flavor your bird prefers before making up an entire batch.)

5. I normally use a maintenance formulation of a compressed parrot pellet for the fourth portion of the diet, because it falls apart easily and tends to coat the other ingredients so the bird ingests more of it. Extruded parrot pellets or dry dog food that have been blenderized can also be used. If using dog food, choose a good quality brand of dry maintenance dog food, such as Science Diet Canine Maintenance or Iams.

6. If fed to small parrot species, or if your bird only picks out one or two ingredients, this diet can be blenderized to improve the homogeneity of the food.

7. Prior to serving, a good quality vitamin-mineral mix and a calcium supplement should be added to each serving portion. I generally use

a sprinkle of Nekton-S or Prime, and add 1 teaspoon of calcium gluconate syrup or a heavy sprinkle of ground oyster shell.

A.B.R.C. Diet

The Avicultural Breeding and Research Center in Florida uses yet another approach to parrot feeding. Their diets consist of seed mix with added poultry layer pellets and small kibble dog food, cuttlebone, red dry peppers, a soft food mash of fruits and vegetables, supplements, and other natural foods such as palm nuts, pandanus fruit, and branches. The types and varieties of foods fed vary with the species involved and the season.

A complete description of the A.B.R.C. diet and its nutritional analysis is provided in the center's recent publication Psittacine Aviculture: Perspectives, Techniques, and Research. (See Useful Literature and Addresses, page 176.)

Lory Diet 1

This is the diet used by the San Diego Zoo in their feeding program, as described by Dr. Gary Gallerstein in his book The Bird Owner's Home Health and Care Handbook (first edition, 1984, Howell Book House Inc., 230 Park Avenue, New York, New York 10169). I have modified it somewhat for the sake of clarity.

Ingredients:
4 apples
4 leaves of Romaine. lettuce, spinach, Swiss chard, or kale
1 carrot
3 ounces (85 g) raisins
1 ounce trout chow
5 ounces sugar
2–3 ounces (57–85 g) cooked rice
2 ounces millet
1/4 of the milk and meat of 1 coconut
1 teaspoon Lory Premix (available from Zeigler Brothers, P.O. Box 95, Gardners, Pennsylvania 17324)

Directions:
1. Combine and blenderize all the ingredients until the mixture resembles a thick applesauce.

2. If the mixture is too thick, small amounts of boiled water can be added until it reaches the desired consistency.

3. Freeze individual portions in small plastic bags and thaw as needed.

4. Supplement with a variety of other fruits and vegetables, seeds, or live insects depending on the species of bird.

Lory Diet 2

This recipe, which was suggested to me by Dr. Matthew Vriends, makes use of several commercially available products. This may make things easier or more difficult depending on the availability of these items in your area.

70% "Lories Delight" Dry Diet
15% Avico's "Lory Life" Nectar
15% fresh fruit and green food salad

1. "Lories Delight" Dry Food is available from John Vanderhoof, P.O. Box 575, Woodlake, California 93286.

2. Avico's "Lory Life" Nectar is available from Cuttlebone Plus, P.O. Box 305, Fallbrook, California 92028.

3. The fresh fruit and green food salad can consist of items such as apples, pears, peaches, pineapples, strawberries, seedless grapes, carrots, kale, endive, Swiss chard, and spinach.

4. In addition to this as the basic diet, the diet can be supplemented daily with L/M's Canary, Finch, and Softbill-Plus (available from L/M Animal Farms, Pleasant Plain, Ohio 45162), as well as live insects or grains depending on the species of bird.

Basic Soft-bill Diet

This is a recipe I found years ago recommended by Aves International. Recent changes in bird feeding practices and an improvement in the quality of avian supplements has resulted in my modifying it somewhat in order to update it.

Ingredients:
2 parts apples
1 part carrots
2 parts monkey chow
Good quality avian vitamin/mineral supplement, kelp powder, ground cuttlebone

Directions:

1. The kelp powder is available in health food stores. For this recipe, I prefer Hagen's Prime vitamin/mineral mix. Cuttlebone is available in pet stores. Add a sprinkle of each to the mix and blenderize.

2. It is important that this basic diet is supplemented with a variety of other food items depending on the breed of soft-bill bird involved. For example, frugivores such as touracos or fruit pigeons can be supplemented with other chopped fruits and greens. Nectivores such as sunbirds and honeycreepers, which prefer a more liquid diet, can have one part of the basic recipe mixed with two parts artificial nectar. Insectivores should be provided with additional live insects.

Chapter 11
Specialty Foods

Raising Insects

As we have discussed, seed-only diets are deficient in many important nutrients. Yet we also know that, at least for the smaller species of seed eaters, such as the finches and for many of the soft-bills, the present commercially available diets do not seem to supply all the nutrients these birds require. Many of these species seem to need live food in order to remain healthy and breed successfully.

Finches can benefit from the inclusion of insects in their diet.

Several different insects can be purchased or raised successfully at home in order to meet these needs. Mealworms, crickets, fruit flies, fly larvae, and tubifex worms are just some examples of insects that can be raised at home or purchased from your local pet store. One company, Nekton, produces a number of different insect-breeding concentrates in order to make insect-raising at home even easier. It should be noted that garden bugs and grubs may carry parasites that can be harmful, if not deadly, to your bird. Cockroaches are not acceptable food sources because of the parasites they may contain. If you do feed garden bugs and grubs, you should have a stool sample examined every two months by your avian veterinarian to make sure no intestinal parasites are present.

Larger birds such as toucans and mynahs also enjoy the occasional "pinkie" (hairless) mouse, which can also be purchased at your local pet store.

If your pet store does not stock live foods, they can supply you with the names and numbers of several companies that do. Many of these companies can ship live food to you directly, particularly mealworms and crickets.

Raising Mealworms

One of the easiest and cleanest insects to raise at home is the mealworm. All that is required is some initial stock, raw bran and oatmeal, a few chunks of raw potato or carrot, some plastic dishpan-sized containers, some screening, and some patience.

Begin by mixing 1 part oatmeal to 3 parts raw bran. Place a layer 1 inch (2.5 cm) deep into each dishpan, and add 1 raw potato or 1 raw carrot cut into 2-inch (5 cm) chunks. Keep the dishpans in an area of your home that remains at a constant 60°F (15.6°C). To each dishpan, add a few of your initial mealworm stock. Cover the dishpan with screening material to keep the mealworms in and vermin out. You can begin with any stage of mealworm; the only variation will be in the length of time it takes for the mealworms to reproduce.

If you begin with mealworm larvae, the larvae will eat and grow until they go into the quiescent phase called the pupae. After several weeks, the pupae will develop into beetles. These beetles are initially cream colored, but darken to brown several hours after hatching. It is these beetles that lay the eggs that hatch into mealworm larvae, thereby completing the cycle. The time between the appearance of the beetles and the development of the larvae that can be harvested and fed is between six to eight weeks.

It is important to keep the media moist, particularly after the appearance of the larvae. Therefore, potato or carrot slices should be replaced regularly, at least once a week. As the larvae grow and work the medium, the bran begins to take on a flourlike consistency. At this point fresh oatmeal-raw bran should be added to the mixture, or the insects can be sifted out with a kitchen strainer and set up in a new container. Keep the old container for one month to harvest any eggs and small larvae that have since hatched and grown that were not collected on the first straining. Alternatively, after one complete cycle 20 to 30 larvae can be saved from the batch and set up in a fresh tub of medium to continue the cycle. With three or four tubs on the go, it is possible to have fresh mealworm larvae available all year-round.

Once the larvae have reached the desired size, they can be cooled to between 45 to 52°F (7–11°C). At this temperature they will become dormant and can be kept for several months.

It is best to feed mealworms that are plump and white, particularly to small or young birds. The brown shell of the older larvae contains a great deal of chitin that can be harder to digest and may cause constipation.

Raising Crickets and Locusts

Crickets can be raised in much the same way as mealworms, with a few important differences. Crickets require a moister environment and a dark place to hide. Most people use a glass aquarium with a few inches of oatmeal-bran medium, a few broken and inverted cardboard egg cartons, and a layer of leafy vegetables, such as Romaine lettuce, to provide sufficient moisture. Locusts can be raised in much the same way, although they require a warm temperature of at least 81°F (27°C). This can be achieved by using an overhead incandescent light bulb to warm the aquarium.

These insects must have their hind legs cut or removed prior to feeding so that they do not escape from the bird's cage and into your home.

Raising Fruit Flies

Fruit flies are extremely easy to raise; they appear to gather almost immediately in the presence of rotting fruit. You can begin by placing a piece of ripe fruit in a jar covered with a wide mesh screen and leaving it outside for a day in the summer or early fall. (It is important that the screening be of a wide enough mesh to let in the fruit flies, but not large enough for regular flies or wasps.) The fruit flies are attracted by the smell of the ripe fruit and enter the jar. At this point you can place a tight mesh screen on the jar, or close the jar completely, and add fresh fruit as required. The jar should be opened and the insects fed to your birds every few days.

One of my owners used to keep hummingbirds flying free in his living room. As a treat, he would often offer them fruit flies. As soon as he entered the room with the fruit-fly jar the birds would gather around him, snatching the fruit flies up as they flew out of the jar.

Despite his experience, fruit flies can be a nuisance if they get free in your home, so many people only feed them to birds in outdoor aviaries. In this case, you can place a piece of fruit in a dish with the more open wire mesh. The mesh will keep your birds from consuming the overripe fruit, but they can eat the fruit flies as they come out through the mesh. (Naturally, this technique may not work well if you are plagued with heavy populations of wasps.)

Dehydrating Fruit

Although feeding fresh fruit is preferable, limited seasonal availability sometimes makes this difficult. One idea that may have some use is to dehydrate fruit. It is best to dehydrate fruit yourself rather than purchase these products, because they tend to be expensive and are treated with sulfur or preservatives that your bird need not consume.

Fruit can be dehydrated in the oven, although this method does use a lot of energy and is inefficient. In this case, an electric oven is set at 143°F (62°C). The sliced fruit is placed on trays, the oven door is left slightly ajar, and a fan is placed outside the oven to keep the air circulating to aid in the drying process. This method takes several hours and is not really recommended.

If the thought of dehydrating fruit appeals to you, than it is best to invest in a good quality commercial dehydrator. Not only can this provide healthy snacks for your pet birds, but it will also provide a healthy source of snacks for you!

Rather than using a commercial product to prevent the fruit from browning, dipping the fruit in a mixture of 1 tablespoon of lemon juice to 1/2 cup of water works very well.

Although instructions vary with each machine, several tips apply to all. Do not mix fruits and vegetables in one drying load; the flavors combine, producing a product that is neither one nor the other. Be sure to allow the food to cool before removing it from the dehydrator and storing it. Store the food in airtight containers; if the fruit is not dehydrated enough, or is improperly stored, mold will form. Moldy food should be discarded.

Apples, apricots, strawberries, bananas, pears, peaches, and watermelon are all fruits that can be dehydrated and fed as treats when fresh fruits are not available. Instructions for the preparation of each of these items should be included with your dehydrator.

Seeds

The inclusion of seeds in the Specialty Foods chapter is a deliberate one; although many pet bird books say that seeds should not form the entire diet, they invariably go on to describe the seed portion of the diet in great detail, and gloss over the discussion of suitable vegetables, fruits, animal proteins, and pelleted rations. It is hoped that by placing seeds in this category it will drive home the message that seed feeding should be deemphasized in pet bird nutrition, in favor of a broader, more varied, and more nutritionally balanced feeding regimen. Nonetheless, seeds do contain many worthwhile nutrients, and to ignore them altogether would do a disservice to this useful food source.

An example of a seed mix for finches.

In the wild, birds forage for many different types of ripening seeds and grasses at different times of the year. This natural variety helps to balance the vitamin, mineral, and amino acid deficiencies that may exist in any one seed type. In the same way, offering a variety of seeds in a seed mix will help offset some of the deficiencies that exist in each seed type, although we know that no seed diet can provide a completely balanced ration. Many of the seeds we now consider standard in seed mixes are not seeds native to the bird's original habitat. This is all the more reason why we should choose as wide a variety of seeds as possible in the seed mix, and why we should also try to choose seeds that are closer in composition to those seeds that the bird would eat in the wild. In other words, just saying a particular species eats seeds as part of its natural diet is not sufficient, particularly for a serious aviculturist attempting to breed that species. One should actually determine which seeds the bird eats in the wild, and try to provide a commonly available seed with a similar carbohydrate, fat, and protein composition.

Size should also be considered in seed mix selection; finches, for example, need a seed mix that contains smaller-sized seeds than those needed for a budgerigar or cockatiel.

The quality of the seed is the most important criterion in seed mix selection; because of the way they are processed, cleaned, and stored, there is a high risk of contamination in seeds. The seeds should be clean, fresh, and dust-free, without foreign objects such as stones, stems, and empty hulls. Seeds, especially sunflower seeds, should be examined for small holes that may indicate the presence of the larvae of seed moths. The presence of webbing also indicates the presence of seed moths. The seed should also be examined closely for grain bugs, a small brown insect that can quickly spread to all the grain products in your home if not controlled. Open hulls, dust, mold, or even a moldy smell indicate older seed, heat exposure, and poor storage conditions and should never be fed to pet birds. You should also never purchase seed from open, uncovered bins or from places where the open seed has been exposed to other birds. This seed may be contaminated with insects and rodent droppings, or even with airborne disease-causing agents from other birds.

Remember that seeds are a perishable food source; old seeds are no more nutritionally valuable than three-month-old potatoes or bread. The very process of drying and storing seeds results in the loss of much of the nutrients available from the same plant in the wild. One indicator of seed freshness is the ability of the seed to sprout. A plastic or ceramic saucer is covered with a wet paper towel. Some seeds are placed on the saucer, and the paper towel is kept moist. Fresh seed should begin to sprout within 24 hours, and by the fourth day, 75 percent of the seed should be sprouted. Seeds that do not pass this test are too old and should be discarded. Seeds should be fed within two months from the date of purchase, and stored in cool, dry conditions in covered, moisture-proof containers. Keeping seed in the refrigerator or freezer will help prolong its shelf life.

Always remember to store seed and other grain products in containers that are insect- and rodent-proof. In this way, even food that is contaminated with insects will not be able to release the insects into the rest of your foodstuffs. This is a wise precaution even with regular human products; I have seen plain rolled oats from a leading, reputable manufacturer that were offered for human consumption that were contaminated with grain bugs. These bugs subsequently spread throughout the rest of the grain products the owners kept in the same cupboard, and it took months of effort to finally eliminate them all.

Seeds are basically divided into two groups: oil or starch seeds. Starch seeds include millet, canary seed, wheat, oats, buckwheat, rice, milo, and corn. They contain less protein than the oil seeds, and also contain a protein of lower biological value than the oil seeds. They are good sources of carbohydrate, and

contain vitamin E and several of the B group vitamins, but they are lacking in vitamins C and D, and in carotene (with the exception of corn, which does contain carotene). The oil seeds include flax, hemp, niger, poppy, peanut, rape, and sesame. Aside from their higher fat content, they are also higher in protein. The following is a list of the most commonly used seeds in pet bird mixes, and some information about their use and nutritive value.

Canary Seed

This seed was originally from the Canary Islands, but it is now cultivated in the United States and Canada. It forms a large part of most canary seed mixes, and is also common in budgerigar and cockatiel seed mixes. It is a low-fat, high-carbohydrate grain that is low in the essential amino acids lysine and methionine.

Millet

There are at least five varieties of millet that are used in pet bird seed mixes. Millet is a low-fat, high-carbohydrate grain. White proso millet is the largest of the common varieties, and is used in canary, budgerigar, cockatiel, and small hookbill diets. It is grown in South Dakota and Colorado. It is deficient in tryptophan. Red millet is slightly smaller, and is often used in finch diets, although it can be used in any small hookbill diet. Yellow panicum, also known as golden millet, is quite small in size and is common in finch diets. Spray millet is often fed as a treat to almost all species of hookbills. It is low in arginine. Millets are grown primarily in Asia and West Africa.

Oats

The hulls of the oat grain may comprise 28 to 45 percent of the weight of grain, therefore most of the oats in pet bird mixes or in treat mixes are hulled, and are referred to as oat groats. They are highly digestible, and are often a favorite of budgerigars. Oats are produced in Europe and the United States. Oats are deficient in methionine, histidine, tryptophan, and lysine.

Buckwheat

Buckwheat is a common component in pigeon seed rations, but should not be offered at more than 5 percent of the ration because the fiber content of its shell is about 10 percent. If available, buckwheat groats can be substituted to avoid this excessive fiber intake.

Examples of some common seeds. Clockwise from the top: striped sunflower seed, hemp seed, oats, canary grass seed, flax seed, white millet, buck wheat, and safflower seed; center: rape seed.

Hard Corn

Although hard corn is often present in large hookbill seed mixes, I find that most birds ignore it, yet the same birds thoroughly enjoy fresh corn. Because fresh corn also has more nutritive value, I tend not to choose a mix with hard corn in favor of offering corn as a fresh food source. Corn is low in the essential amino acid tryptophan. Care must be taken never to feed moldy corn; it may contain the fungus Aspergillus, which can have serious health consequences for pet birds.

Anise

Anise seed is a member of the parsley family, and was originally native to Egypt, although it is now widely cultivated in India, Turkey, Mexico, and Chile. It is a very fragrant seed, and is often added to treat mixes, imparting a licorice odor. It is high in fat content.

Poppy

Poppy seed is often found in treat mixes. It is native to Europe and Asia, but is now cultivated in many countries. It is high in fat content.

Sesame

Sesame seed is high in good quality protein, methionine, and tryptophan, but it lacks the essential amino acid lysine. It is also high in fat content. Sesame seed is primarily grown in India. It is sometimes used in budgerigar seed mixes, and is often found in treat mixes.

Flax

Flax seed comes from the linseed plant. It is high in fat content and deficient in lysine. Flax is grown in Argentina, Canada, India, and the midwestern United States. It is often used in treat mixes.

Hemp

Hemp seeds are high in protein, and are commonly fed in Europe in canary and finch mixes. This is one seed type that should fail your seed sprouting test, because hemp must be sterilized in order to be sold legally in this country. Hemp is primarily imported from Europe and China. It is high in fat content. Soaking the seeds is often recommended to soften the shells a little.

Niger

Niger is a member of the African thistle family and is imported from Ethiopia and India. Finches and canaries appear particularly fond of this seed, and it is often present in treat mixes. It is high in fat content.

Peanuts

Peanuts are legumes. Grown in North Carolina, Virginia, and Texas, they are high in fat content, and are often a favorite of the larger parrot species. Peanuts are deficient in lysine, threonine, methionine, and cysteine. Peanuts are susceptible to the mold Aspergillus flavus, which produces a potent toxin. Thus peanuts should be examined carefully prior to feeding to prevent this important potential source of toxicity.

Rapeseed

This high-fat seed is often included in canary and finch mixes. Its goitrogenic nature is discussed further in the chapter on toxins. The Tower variety, grown in Canada, is considered the best type, because it is low in erucic acid and glucosinolate, substances that are considered toxic for birds.

Safflower

Safflower is high in fat content, and low in the essential amino acid tryptophan. It is quite similar in nutrient composition to sunflower seed, so that advertising claims of "no sunflower" seed are not beneficial if the bird substitutes safflower for its previous sunflower seed habits. However, safflower seed is more difficult to hull and contains a bitter resin that has some cathartic properties, so that birds tend to eat less of this seed than they do of sunflower seeds. It is grown primarily in California.

Sunflower

For many years a rumor has persisted that sunflower seeds contain an addictive substance. This is not true, yet the term "sunflower seed addict" is a valid description of what many pet bird owners observe; these birds eat sunflower seeds to the exclusion of all other dietary ingredients offered. There are two reasons for this apparent addiction: first, the high fat content of these seeds make them highly palatable; second, the cracking open of the sunflower seed provides "occupational therapy," a displacement behavior to help deal with the stress of captivity in an unstimulating environment.

There are several species of sunflower seed commonly used in seed mixes. The smaller black seeds often seen in wild bird mixes are harder to hull and appear less satisfying than the larger, striped variety. In terms of the striped varieties, there appears to be no major difference in terms of nutritional composition between the kernel of gray-striped and black-striped varieties, despite rumors to the contrary. Although it is true that the gray-striped variety grown in California has a larger hull, the black-striped variety grown in the midwestern United States has the same kernel size and nutritive value, and is often cheaper and has less bacterial contamination than the gray-striped type. All sunflower seeds are high in fat content and low in the essential amino acid tryptophan.

Treat Mixes

An amazing selection of treat foods are available commercially for a wide variety of pet birds, particularly those in the canary and finch families. These treats include fruit mixes, vegetable mixes, song food, molting food, breeding food, egg food, nesting food, various shaped seed items, and color enhancement products, just to name a few.

These products can add variety and interest to your bird's diet, and can generally be recommended, provided they are used as treats and supplied in small quantities— no more than 5 percent of the diet per day. One way to add greater variety is to mix three or four different products together, and offer a small treat cup of the combination.

Many of these products contain dehydrated fruits and vegetables, and seeds that are known to have a higher fat and higher protein content than regular seed mixes. These seeds have been used traditionally because it was believed that the higher protein content in these seeds would supply the protein needed for growing new feathers during a molt or for the egg during egg production. However, as you know from our discussion so far, no matter how rich the seed, it still cannot provide all the nutrients required for feather formation or reproduction because seeds as a group lack certain essential nutrients. For this reason these mixes can only be viewed as a supplement and not as a complete diet.

I used to have a personal prejudice against many of the seeds-stuck-on-stick-type treat products, mainly because I didn't feel they were much different than a regular seed mix to which a sweetener has been added to "glue" the seeds together. Some of these products have now been improved, however, and can provide beak exercise and mental stimulation as the bird tries to wrestle the food from the stick. Choose those products that contain fruits, vegetables, or nuts, in addition to the usual seeds. One of the better of these products is Lafeber's Nutri-Berries. These are a combination of seeds, essential amino acids, vitamins, and minerals, and can be very useful in getting a stubborn, "seed-only" budgerigar or cockatiel to sample a better balanced ration. Once the bird has started trying these, it is easier to switch to other alternatives, such as some of the muffin recipes described below, or the "seed-plus-pellet" biscuits that are also on the market.

Various commercial or home-made egg foods can be useful during the reproduction cycle, or during times of metabolic stress such as molting or illness. Although egg is considered the most biologically available protein, egg yolk is high in cholesterol and can result in a long-term clogging of the arteries in birds just as it can in people. For this reason the entire egg should be used in egg food formulation, and it should only be used daily during times of reproduction. At other times it should not be offered more than once or twice a week.

There are various color enhancement products available, but the most common of these are the products that are produced to bring out the red color in red-factor canaries. Color enhancement products may contain high levels of yellow beta carotene, and are designed to improve the color of yellow, green, and blue feathers. Flamen oil and canthaxanthin are designed to improve the color of red feathers.

With all of these products, keeping them in airtight containers in the refrigerator will prolong their shelf life.

Other Recipes

It never ceases to amaze me how some birds would never touch a fruit or vegetable, but will eat a piece of bread. For these birds, baking nutritious cakes or muffins is an ideal way to fool them into eating a better diet. Below is a list of several recipes I have gathered from various sources over the years.

Banana Nut Muffins
Ingredients:
  2 cups whole wheat flour
  2/3 cup sugar
  1 teaspoon baking powder
  1 teaspoon baking soda
  1/4 teaspoon salt
  1/4 cup cheddar cheese
  3/4 cup chopped bananas
  1/2 cup nuts, finely chopped
  2 eggs with shell
  1/2 cup vegetable oil

Directions:
  Mix the dry ingredients in a bowl. Wash the eggs thoroughly, blenderize including the shell, add the oil, and mix well. Add the eggs and oil to the dry ingredients. Spoon into greased muffin cups. Bake for 20 to 25 minutes in a 375°F (190°C) oven,

or until a toothpick inserted in the center comes out clean.

Apple-Cheese Muffins

Ingredients:
- 2 cups whole wheat flour
- 1 1/2 teaspoons baking powder
- 1/2 teaspoon baking soda
- 1 teaspoon salt
- 1/2 cup shredded cheddar cheese
- 1/2 cup butter, softened
- 1/3 cup sugar
- 2 eggs with shells
- 1/2 cup chopped apple
- 1/2 cup shredded carrot

Directions:

Mix the first five ingredients together in a bowl. Wash the eggs, then blenderize the eggs with the shell included. Add butter, sugar, apple, and carrot to the eggs and blenderize briefly to mix. Stir together with the dry ingredients until just combined. Spoon into greased muffin tins and bake at 350°F (175°) for 20 to 25 minutes, or until springy to the touch.

Sweet Potato Muffins

Ingredients:
- 1 cup all-purpose flour
- 3/4 cup whole wheat flour
- 1 teaspoon salt
- 1 tablespoon baking powder
- 1 tablespoon brown sugar
- 1/2 cup coarsely chopped nuts
- 1/2 cup chopped dates
- 2 eggs with shells
- 3/4 cup milk
- 1 cup cooked mashed sweet potatoes
- 1/4 cup melted butter

Directions:

Mix the first seven ingredients together. Wash eggs and blenderize, including the shells. Add the egg to the remaining moist ingredients and stir. Stir together with dry ingredients until just combined. Spoon into greased muffin tins and bake at 425°F (220°C) for about 25 minutes, or until springy to the touch.

Birdie French Toast

Ingredients:
- 1 slice whole wheat bread
- 1 egg
- 2 teaspoons milk
- 1/4 cup millet seeds

Directions:

This is a useful recipe for those hard to convert seed-eating budgies. Beat the egg and milk together. Dip the bread into the egg mixture to coat it, then sprinkle with millet seeds. Fry in 2 tablespoons vegetable oil in an iron frying pan and serve when cooled. A dash of onion powder, chili powder, or marjoram can be added to the egg if you have discovered your bird likes these flavors.

Roger Harlin's Bean Casserole

Ingredients:
- 1 can low-salt corn
- 1 can low-salt green peas
- 1 can red kidney beans
- 3/4 cup macaroni

Directions:

Pour the entire can contents into a saucepan and heat until boiling.

Add sufficient macaroni to soak up the moisture, and cook for 7 to 10 minutes or until the macaroni is done. Depending on the amount of water in the brand of canned vegetables you are using, you may need to add water in order to completely cook the macaroni. Baby lima beans can be used instead of red kidney beans, and cheese can be melted over the top just before serving.

Color Food
(Dee Hedberg's Recipe)
Ingredients:
- 4 cups Wheatena
- 2 cups wheat germ
- 2 cups wheat hearts
- 8 cups oatmeal
- 4 tablespoons Flamen oil (available in pet stores)
- 4 tablespoons Linatone (available in pet stores)

Directions:
Mix all of the ingredients together thoroughly and freeze in individual portions. Thaw as needed. Mix with grated carrots just before serving. (Recipe given in Bird Talk, August, 1988; author Pamela Higdon.)

Egg Food
Ingredients:
- 1 hard-boiled egg with shell
- 2 tablespoons bread crumbs
- 2 tablespoons pablum
- 1 teaspoon dried powdered milk
- 1/2 teaspoon soy protein isolate (available in health food stores)
- 1/2 teaspoon avian vitamin/mineral mix
- 1/4 teaspoon finely ground oyster shell

Directions:
Process the egg until finely mashed. Add the egg to the remaining ingredients. The final mixture should be soft, crumbly, and fluffy. If it is too moist, add equal portions of bread crumbs and pablum until the desired consistency is reached. Freeze in individual portions, and thaw as needed.

Other Products

A number of products are now available commercially that can be useful in developing a well-balanced diet, aside from the pelleted rations that are recommended and that are discussed elsewhere in the book. Most of these products are available through mail order from various bird magazines such as *Bird Talk* and *Bird World* (see Useful Literature and Addresses, page 176), whereas others are readily available in pet stores. Just a few of these products are listed below to give you some idea of what is currently available, although new products are being introduced all the time.

For Lories
- Avico's Lory and Softbill Diets, Lory Life, Lory Life Nectar, c/o Cuttlebone Plus, P.O. Box 305, Fallbrook, California 92028. Tel. (619) 731-2242.
- CéDé Lori/Hand-feeding Diets, c/o Sunshine Bird Supplies Inc.,

8535 N.W. 56th Street, Miami, Florida 33166. Tel. (305) 593-2666.

• L/M's Canary, Finch, and Softbill Plus, c/o L/M Animal Farms, Pleasant Plain, Ohio 45162. Tel. (800) 354-0407.

• Lories' Delight Dry Diet, c/o J. Vanderhoof, P.O. Box 575, Woodlake, California 93286. Tel. (209) 564-3610.

• Nekton-Lori, c/o Nekton USA, 14405-60th Street N., Clearwater, Florida 34620. Tel. (813) 530-3500.

• Roudybush Nectar Diets, c/o Roudybush Inc., Box 908, Templeton, California 93465. Tel. (800) 326-1726.

Pasta/Vegetable Mixes

• Birdy Banquet, c/o Pretty Bird International, Inc., 5810 Stacy Trail, Stacy, Minnesota 55079. Tel. (800) 356-5020.

• Noodles N Nuts, Original Corn Bean Mix, Rainforest Rice Pudding, c/o Crazy Corn, 13330 Bessemer St., Van Nuys, California 91401. Tel. (818) 997-0598.

For Seed Junkies

• Birdy Bread and Muffin Mix, c/o Pretty Bird International, Inc., 5810 Stacy Trail, Stacy, Minnesota 55079. Tel. (800) 356-5020.

• Dr. D's Spicey Treats, c/o Avi Sci, Inc., P.O. Box 598, Okemos, Michigan. Tel. (800) 942-3438.

• Nutri-Berries, Avi-Cakes, c/o Lafeber Co. R.R # 2, Odell, Illinois 60460. Tel. (800) 842-6445.

• Peck n' Coo Biscuits; Bits O' Fruit and Nuts, Hot Chilis and Corn, Veggie, Peanut Butter, Protein-Plus, c/o D.D. Pet Products, P.O. Box 7305, Arlington, Virginia 22207. Tel. (703) 532-3983.

Chapter 12
Food Additives

Food additives are substances that are added to food during processing in order to retain or improve its desired characteristics or quality. Additives may enhance the color, flavor, texture, or appearance of food, retain or increase its nutritive value, and prevent microbial spoilage or oxidative changes. There are dozens of these products in use in human food preparation, and we need not discuss all of them here. The substances described here are those in most common use in avian diets.

Preservatives

As I have stated before, bird feed is a perishable foodstuff, therefore the use of preservatives is a common practice, just as it is for our own foodstuffs. There are some pelleted feed manufacturers that choose not to use preservatives. With these feeds it is essential to test the food regularly before offering it for freshness, although this practice is good advice for any food.

There are two types of preservatives in common use in avian feeds, namely antioxidants and antimicrobials. Antioxidants are substances that prevent oxygen from interacting with the foodstuff and oxidizing it. The brown discoloration that occurs when the cut surface of an apple is exposed to the air is an example of oxidation. Examples of antioxidants include ascorbic acid (vitamin C), sodium ascorbate, tocopherol (vitamin E), lecithin, butylated hydroxyanisole (BHA), butylated hydroxytoluene (BHT), sulfur dioxide, sulfites, and ethoxyquin. Ethoxyquin and BHT are antioxidants in common use in the pet food industry. There was a rumor several years ago that these feed additives have detrimental effects. However, feeding trials on dogs failed to confirm that any detrimental effects could be attributed to the use of these products, and the controversy died down. There is still a concern in the general public that these substances may be harmful in some way, although in what way is not known. It is known that some people are allergic to sulfur compounds; for these people, sulfur dioxide and sulfites are harmful. It is not known whether a similar allergic reaction is possible in pet birds.

Flushing the food with an inert gas, such as nitrogen or carbon dioxide, before packing it in airtight sealed packages is another way to achieve an antioxidant effect without adding a chemical substance to the food. This is actually a very good method; as well as its antioxidant function, this type of packaging also helps to prevent insect contamination prior to purchase.

The second category of food preservatives is the antimicrobials. These are the substances that help to prevent the development of molds, yeasts, and bacteria in foods. Good sanitation practices go a long way in avoiding food contamination with these microbial organisms, nonetheless, antimicrobials are often used. Antimicrobial substances include benzoic acid, sodium benzoate, sorbic acid, sorbates, calcium proprionate, and sodium diacetate. These substances have been used for many years in human food preparation without apparent ill effects.

Artificial and Natural Flavors and Colors

Artificial and natural flavors and colors are used commonly in pet bird diet formulations, and to date no evidence has shown that these substances are harmful to these species. In humans, there is some evidence to suggest that certain artificial flavors, colors, or food additives may cause allergic reactions or contribute to hyperactivity in some people. For this reason, some manufacturers have produced pelleted rations that do not contain artificial flavors or colors. Whether you choose to use these products is somewhat of a matter of personal taste and opinion; it is important to recognize, however, that these products are more expensive to produce due to the quality of the ingredients, and therefore the cost of these foods are a little higher than some other products.

A number of seed manufacturers have begun adding artificial colors to their seed mixes, and are charging a premium for these products. Although this may make the food more visually appealing, this practice is considered primarily cosmetic and is not considered to improve the quality of the food. When choosing a product, make sure that the food is actually nutritionally sound; do not be deceived by coloring.

Color-feeding

Color-feeding refers to the practice of feeding foods high in carotenes in order to achieve brighter colored feathers in pet birds.

Color-feeding should begin several weeks before the molt in order to produce even feather coloration. Baby birds need to begin color-feeding at six weeks of age in order to prepare for their first molt at eight to ten weeks of age.

Yellow canaries produce their color from the yellow carotenoid pigment xanthophyll, found in rape, thistle, hemp, and dark green foods such as kale and dandelion leaves.

As mentioned in the chapter on breed specifics, red-factor canaries are a result of genetics. Nonetheless, their color can be enhanced by certain foodstuffs. Natural pigment is found in those foodstuffs high in beta carotene, such as carrots, sweet red peppers, and paprika. Foodstuffs that contain high levels of yellow carotenoids will dilute the red coloration, and should therefore be decreased if a bright red color is desired in a red-factor canary. For example, egg yolk, canary seed, rapeseed, and dark green vegetables should be replaced with carrot, oats, niger, and red berries in order to increase the beta carotene and decrease the yellow carotenoid levels in the diet.

There are several color-enhancement products that are available commercially. Yellow beta carotene is a specific yellow carotenoid that will enhance the colors of any bird, particularly the yellows, blues, and greens. Flamen oil is a blend of dark red carrot oil and other vegetable oils high in vitamins D, E, and

Color-feeding enhances the color of red-factor canaries.

carotene. Canthaxanthin is a synthetic product fed to red-factor canaries to optimize their color. This product should be measured and applied only according to the manufacturer's recommendations, because excess supplementation will result in an unattractive brownish tint to the feathers rather than the desired shade of red. Feeding this product to a yellow canary will produce an orange bird, but will not produce the deep red color that can be achieved in a red-factor bird.

In order to achieve the best coloration possible in a red-factor canary, a blend of beta carotene and canthaxanthin is required. The exact proportions of these substances used varies with the breeder, and is a common topic of conversation among canary fanciers.

Probiotics

Probiotics are beneficial bacteria that have been added to certain products in an effort to suppress the growth of potential disease-causing organisms. The most common of the organisms used is Lactobacillus acidophilus, the same bacteria that is present in yogurt. Although this is not the same Lactobacillus organism that normally inhabits the crop, it is believed that this organism may produce metabolites that help to acidify the crop contents. It is believed that acidifying the crop contents somewhat helps to maintain the optimum conditions for the normal crop flora, and inhibits the growth of pathogenic yeast organisms.

Digestive Enzymes

Dietary supplementation of digestive enzymes in hand-fed birds has been advocated as a way to aid digestion and to stimulate weight gain and feed conversion. A study was performed on hand-fed Eclectus parrots at the Avicultural Breeding and Research Center in order to test the validity of this practice. Their study showed that there were absolutely no observable differences in growth weight or weight gain between birds that were or were not supplemented, thus calling into question the validity of the practice. Although I do not question the results of the study, I must confess that the results surprise me. It is well known that the levels of digestive enzymes are low in newly hatched chicks and turkey poults,

so one would expect that adding digestive enzymes might improve the digestibility of certain nutrients aiding in their absorption. Further research is needed to explain why this does not appear to occur in the feeding trial that was done.

Vitamin and Mineral Mixes

There are several good quality vitamin/mineral mixes currently on the market. Some of these products are in liquid form, although many of the newer products come in a powder. The powdered products are believed to be more stable, but they are subject to damage by high humidity levels. When using powdered products, it is good advice to put a few tablespoonsful in a salt shaker, and keep the remaining product in a tightly closed container in the refrigerator to prolong its shelf life.

There is some controversy concerning whether adding a vitamin/mineral mix to the water is beneficial or harmful. Those against the practice claim that the vitamins oxidize quickly in water, thereby losing their potency. They also claim that these products increase the rate of bacterial multiplication in the water. I personally agree that there is some truth to these claims, and it is preferable to sprinkle the substance on a moist foodstuff as opposed to putting it in the drinking water if possible. On the other hand, in stubborn birds that refuse to eat moist foods, adding the mix to the water may be the only way to get the bird to consume the product. In this case, supplementation in the water is better than no supplementation at all, and the practice is not particularly harmful provided the water is changed twice daily and the water cup is properly disinfected.

When selecting a supplement, be sure to choose a product that contains both vitamins and minerals. Some products on the market contain one or the other, thus misleading the purchaser into believing they are providing a complete supplement when they are only providing one component. As stated, the new powdered supplements are considered better than the liquids. Two well-known products currently on the market are Prime (by Hagen) and Nekton-S (Nekton-Produkte). Both products have their relative merits. Nekton-S is more readily soluble in the water, and is useful if water supplementation is the only way you can induce your bird to consume the supplement. Prime is not as water-soluble, and is recommended to be used sprinkled onto soft foods. Prime has a pleasant orange scent, and also contains the amino acids methionine and lysine, which we have already discussed as being deficient in seed diets.

Several seed mixes now claim to be "vitaminized" or "fortified." Although these seeds may be improved somewhat over other mixes, the fact remains that many of these seed mixes are still deficient in several key ingredients, such as certain amino acids, and therefore these seeds cannot be regarded as a complete diet. In some cases the additional vitamins and minerals have only been sprayed onto the seed that is still in the husk. Because birds husk the seed before consuming it, the value of this practice is questionable. Another manufacturer has added its supplement in the form of a coated hulled seed. The chances of the bird consuming these hulled seeds, and thus ingesting the supplement, is greater than with the other method and may be of some benefit.

In general, additional vitamin/mineral supplementation is not required if your bird consumes a pelleted ration on a regular basis, because most of these rations are formulated to contain all the vitamins and minerals needed for health and maintenance.

Mineral Blocks and Cuttlebone

Cuttlebone is derived from the cuttlefish. It is almost completely composed of calcium carbonate, which is a readily available form of calcium. Oyster shell is also a form of calcium carbonate and should be regarded as such, and not

Cuttlebone can be a useful source of calcium carbonate.

considered to be a form of grit, because it is dissolved and absorbed readily from the gizzard.

There are many different mineral blocks on the market. Although all of these blocks contain calcium carbonate, choose a mineral block that also contains zinc, sodium, potassium, magnesium, manganese, copper, iodine, and iron. For budgerigars, it is essential to choose a mineral block that contains added iodine, because goiter resulting from iodine deficiency is a common problem in this species.

Fruit-flavored mineral blocks are a relatively new item on the market, and may be more attractive to some birds than the traditional mineral blocks, thereby encouraging consumption of these important sources of added minerals and calcium.

Chapter 13
Before the Egg

Growth

Before one can even begin to consider reproduction, one must first satisfy the growth requirements of the parent birds. Although many of the smaller breeds reach sexual maturity before the age of two, for most larger species sexual maturity is not reached before three to seven years of age. Now that more species are captive-bred, we can use these first three to seven years to raise a strong, healthy, breeding bird by providing conditions that will optimize growth rates and genetic potential. A large part of optimizing a bird's genetic potential lies in supplying a nutritionally sound diet. It is conceivable that by providing a well balanced diet and a healthy environment we can exceed the conditions available to the bird in the wild, thereby dramatically increasing the life span and reproductive potential of each species.

The years before sexual maturity are the years of the greatest physiological change and metabolic needs. The requirements of all nutrients are high, including the need for sufficient calcium and pro-

Before one can consider reproduction, one must first satisfy the requirements of the adult bird.

tein. Many manufacturers provide diets that are formulated for growth and reproduction, but in some cases these diets may not provide all the nutrients required to optimize the genetic potential of each bird. It will take several generations of breeding and careful record keeping to weed out the truly successful diets from those that are only marginally adequate. Aviculture has made great strides in trying to take an active role in the improvement of bird breeding. It is my hope that this section will stimulate you to keep careful records of your feeding and management practices, so that some day this information can be compiled to improve avicultural techniques worldwide.

Stages of embryo development. Clockwise, from bottom left to bottom right: fresh-laid egg, 5th day, 8th day, 14th day, 17th day. A hatching chick is seen in the center of the drawing.

Reproduction

The captive breeding of parrots is one way in which we can play an active stewardship role in the preservation of many species of birds. The illegal trade in wild-caught parrots, coupled with the habitat destruction occurring globally, has severely decimated many species, putting many of these on the endangered list. Breeding birds domestically has many beneficial effects. First, captive-bred birds are better adapted to captivity and make better pets. Second, an increase in the availability of species from local breeders discourages the illegal trade, thus decreasing the drain on the wild population. Third, if captive breeding is successful, there will eventually be sufficient numbers of birds to return to the wild, once we have learned the value of preserving our fragile ecosystems.

Breeding is a process that requires far more than just a balanced diet. It is a challenging undertaking, requiring time, knowledge, financial investment, and commitment. Before choosing to breed birds yourself, it is wise to work with a reputable breeder or aviculturist for a few years in order to truly understand the challenges and expense involved. By the same token, if you currently own a bird that was originally wild-caught and is known to be on the endangered species list, you should consider whether your bird may be happier in a breeding situation than as a pet, particularly if the bird is not very tame. There are many species currently being bred for which the genetic pool is limited; your bird may provide the genetic material needed to improve the species. This idea has been advocated by several avicultural federations, and may well become a standard practice in the

years to come, as registries for various species are developed.

In terms of nutrition, an important point should be made. For many years it was believed that breeding birds needed to be kept on breeder rations all year. However, it was found that the high levels of protein and calcium led to the development of early kidney disease. It is now known that these birds should only receive these diets for approximately six weeks prior to breeding, and for approximately one month after the chicks have left the nest. This regimen will more closely mimic the seasonal variability in food supply that stimulates reproduction in the first place.

The Egg

The egg is truly a biological miracle. All the material needed to produce an entire bird is contained within it. By the time it is laid, all that is required is to keep it warm and sufficiently humid, and to turn it from time to time. But how does the egg get to this point and how does nutrition play a role? Let's discuss these questions.

Approximately 24 hours pass from the time an oocyte is released from the ovary, until the finished egg is released from the body. The egg yolk, or oocyte, is released from the ovary and picked up by the infundibulum. This is the site of fertilization, and the oocyte spends 15 minutes in this location. The magnum is the site of the secretion of albumen, or egg white, and this process takes approximately three hours. The developing egg then passes into the isthmus, the site of eggshell membrane secretion, where it spends just under two hours. Twenty hours is then spent in the shell gland. This is the site of the addition of fluid to the egg (referred to as "plumping"), the stratification of albumen, and of course the production of the shell itself and any shell pigments (depending on the species). At this time, the egg is ready to be passed.

The process of egg formation is more complex than this simple description implies; the physiological processes involved stagger the imagination. For example, in the chicken, the hen deposits about 2 grams of calcium on the egg in 15 hours. This is the equivalent of removing the total amount of circulating calcium from the bloodstream every 15 minutes for 15 hours. In order to perform this remarkable feat, tremendous changes must occur in the way calcium is handled in the body by female birds. Estrogen plays a major role in stimulating these changes. First, the influence of this hormone causes a rise in the normal circulating levels of calcium from about 10 mg/100 ml of plasma to 25 mg/100 ml. Second, it stimulates the deposition of 4 to 5 g of calcium derived from the diet into the hollow medullary region of the bones. Third, the absorption of calcium from the gut becomes far more efficient with the onset of reproductive activity. Thus, the calcium secreted into the shell gland during egg formation is derived from the blood, and the blood calcium is derived from the food in the gut, and from the deposits laid down previously in the medullary cavity. Because a bird will attempt to produce an eggshell to the detriment of her own body, it is no wonder that egg binding and brittle bones are so common in birds fed calcium-deficient diets. This is to say nothing of all the other nutrients required by the body for hormone production, fluid regulation, and healthy cell functioning needed to produce the various substances present in the egg.

Remember that an egg can be no better than the hen that laid it; if she is deficient in certain nutrients, the egg may be also, leading to infertile eggs, mid-term embryonic death, or congenital deformities. In fact, I believe that some of the deformities we see in the first few days of life may not be due to the hand-feeding formulas we use, but rather to nutritional deficiencies in the parent birds that result in the production of a substandard egg. If you are experiencing problems in the first few days of life, particularly if you are also seeing problems with poor hatchability, and with babies being raised in the nest, step back and examine the health and nutritional status of the parent birds. Also examine your rearing practices and have your birds checked for infectious diseases.

Chapter 14
After the Egg

After the Hatch

One aspect of nutrition that is often overlooked in the newly hatched chick is a discussion of the rapid series of adjustments in nutrient utilization and changes in metabolism the chick must undergo in the first few weeks of life.

For a few days before, and at the time of emergence from their eggs, the chicks have high circulating levels of fat and ketones in their bloodstream. The residual egg yolk in their abdomen acts as a short-term (largely lipid) nutrient supply for a few days, but they must quickly change metabolically from using lipids (fats) as an energy source to using carbohydrates supplied by the parent birds or by the hand-feeding diet. At the same time, the previously unused digestive tract must develop mechanisms to digest large amounts of complex carbohydrates, proteins, and fats. All this must take place within the first week of life if the bird is going to survive, let alone thrive.

In a study of turkey poults (and remember that turkeys and chickens are born in a more advanced state of development than psittacines), it was found that in the first week of life these birds are handicapped by many physiological limitations. These include a slow adjustment to carbohydrate and fat metabolism, maldigestion of carbohydrates, fats, and proteins, and malabsorption of nutrients, as well as a transitory anemia and poor adrenocortical response to stress.

Baby birds must undergo a rapid series of adjustments in metabolism and nutrient utilization in order to survive.

147

Taking all these factors into consideration, it seems incredible that a baby bird survives at all! It also indicates the need for further research into the early digestive processes in psittacine birds if truly superior hand-feeding diets are to be developed.

Parent-feeding

It should be self-evident that baby birds were meant to be raised by parent birds, and not by artificial incubation and hand-rearing. Artificial incubation and hand-rearing are simply our clumsy attempts to mimic what should occur naturally. Yet more and more, we are relying on hand-raising for species propagation. We blame the parent birds for abandoning the eggs or damaging the chicks, but we fail to understand the fundamental reasons for these events; first, no matter how hard we try, we cannot provide birds in captivity with the conditions present in their natural habitat; second, nature never intended for every egg to survive, even under natural conditions.

It is our unwillingness to accept the laws of nature that has created our present dilemma. We cannot return these birds to the wild, because the destruction of their natural habitats threatens their very survival. If we allow these birds to breed naturally under our artificially imposed conditions, greater egg losses are inevitable as these birds learn to adjust not only to the conditions, but to the very process of parenting. In some cases we have accepted this, because we are unable to raise these birds by hand anyway. However, in cases where we have figured out a way to do it ourselves, we are resorting to hand-raising with increasing frequency. Our excuse is that each egg is so precious with so few birds left in the wild that we cannot afford to let nature take its course. This may be true; however, what is equally true is that some of the motivation for hand-raising is to provide more and better quality birds for the pet trade. This is not necessarily wrong, in that supplying birds for the pet trade will help to decrease the drain on the wild population through illegal trade. Nonetheless, we must recognize that birds that have not been raised by their parents and exposed to a natural flock situation will in turn be ill-prepared to raise their own offspring, or even to breed successfully. It is imperative that we recognize this, and make a concerted effort to produce birds that will be able to survive and breed successfully without our intervention if we ever hope to raise birds for release into the wild.

With this in mind, it is important to recognize that parent-raised chicks are more likely exposed to certain diseases than birds in the nursery environment. Yeast and bacterial intestinal infections are more common in parent-raised birds. The organisms, which are transmitted to the chicks from infected parents, are also able to proliferate more readily in the warm, damp conditions present in the nest box. Unlike in the wild where food is always fresh and feces don't accumulate, the aviary situation is cramped, and spoiled food and feces build up readily, acting as a source of pathogenic organisms, and encouraging the presence of insects and rodents. Aside from a good diet, proper sanitation in the aviary is very important in the prevention of nutritionally-related diseases in parent-raised birds.

Hand-feeding

Despite my concerns regarding the future productivity and survival of our hand-raised birds, I side with many aviculturists in accepting the hand-raising of birds as a temporary necessary evil. For this reason, I have devoted an entire section of this book to nutrition and hand-feeding. This section cannot be regarded as a definitive guide to all aspects of hand-feeding; its purpose is to stimulate an awareness of how nutrition plays a role in this practice, and to stimulate you to engage in further research on your own.

To prevent bacterial contamination of food, feeding utensils must be exceptionally clean, and food should never be rewarmed.

Chapter 15
Hand-feeding

Pediatric nutrition is a field of research that is still in its own infancy. Psittacines are altricial; they are born very undeveloped and dependent. Because poultry are precocial, that is, they complete much of their early development in the egg prior to hatching, it is even more difficult to draw parallels between poultry and psittacine hatchlings than it is with adult birds. For this reason, very little was known about psittacine pediatric nutrition until some important research work was carried out in cockatiels in the mid-1980s. This work led to some significant findings regarding various aspects of hand-raising birds, and stimulated others to investigate this area of nutritional research as well.

When to Hand-feed

Hand-feeding baby birds is a time-consuming, exhausting process, so before beginning it is important to be sure that you have the time and the facilities to perform this challenging task. If you are a novice, it would be wisest to begin with a smaller species such as a cockatiel. These birds mature fairly quickly, so that if you discovered you found the process too tiring, at least you could console yourself with knowing that your baby bird will soon be weaned. With large parrots such as macaws, the hand-feeding process can take several months!

Hand-feeding baby birds is a time-consuming, exhausting process.

Seed-eating birds, such as finches, are seldom hand-raised because the chicks are quite small and somewhat more difficult to manipulate. In most cases breeders use Bengalese, otherwise known as society finches, to act as foster parents, although some breeders do successfully hand-raise these smaller species.

Budgerigars are usually parent-raised, but are handled frequently by the time of weaning so that they are hand-tame by the time they go to a new home.

Cockatiels are often hand-raised, either because the parents are inexperienced, or because the parents wish to breed again and want to have the babies out of the nest so that they can begin a new clutch. Most of the scientific research on hand-feeding has been performed on neonatal cockatiels, so that several good-quality hand-feeding formulas are available for this species. These formulas are an excellent way to take the guesswork out of hand-raising, and I advise them for any novice just starting out as a good way to avoid many of the common mistakes that can be made in feeding.

If the parent birds are feeding and brooding well, many breeders leave the babies with the parent birds for the first few weeks. Hard-to-tame birds, such as lovebirds, ringneck parakeets, and red-rumps, imprint more easily on humans if they are the first "parent" they see, so these birds are usually pulled from the nest before their eyes open. Other small psittacines are pulled at two weeks of age, and larger species are pulled and hand-fed beginning at three weeks of age. Most large or rare psittacine species are hand-raised from the time of hatch on up.

Hand-feeding Formulas

Hand-raising parrots is an art as well as a science, and a plethora of different hand-feeding formulas exist. Some are commercially available, and others were created by innovative aviculturists decades ago, and are still in common use. Which formula is right for your species of bird depends on a number of factors, including how familiar and comfortable you are with preparing the diet, the availability of the dietary components in your area, the diets' actual nutrient composition, and the specific nutritional requirements of your species of parrot. Each diet has its supporters and critics, and my general advice is to confer with other breeders until more scientific research is available for your particular species. Nonetheless, I will provide suggestions and a number of diets to give you some idea of how to begin.

A few hand-feeding formulas are given in Chapter 18, pages 173–175; for more detailed references, see page 176.

Chapter 16

Factors of Importance in Hand-feeding

Environmental Temperature

Environmental temperature has such a profound effect on the metabolism of diet that it is the first issue that should be addressed in this discussion. Various breeders' experiences have resulted in the development of guidelines for environmental temperature based on the hatchling's age. Hatchlings should be kept at 90 to 96°F (32–35°C) for the first three to four days and at 90 to 93°F (32–33.8°C) for the next seven days; early pin feathers (approximately the next two weeks) should be kept at 86 to 90°F (30–32°C); and partial pin feathers to fully feathered (the next three weeks) should be kept at 78 to 86°F (26–30°C).

These temperature recommendations are guidelines, and must be adjusted according to the needs of each individual. A comfortable baby will rest peacefully. If chicks are kept too warm, hyperthermia and death can result; panting, unrest, red skin, vomiting, hyperactivity, and poor growth rate may be less marked signs. Too cold an environmental temperature can lead to poor gut motility, crop stasis, digestive disorders, failure to beg for food, inactivity, shivering, and chicks that are pale and cold to the touch.

Many people make the mistake of keeping babies too warm, with too low an environmental humidity level. (Humidity levels should be 50 to 75 percent.) Too low an environmental humidity level will cause dehydration, which can result in death. In the wild, the nest is usually located in a tree trunk in the humid environment of more tropical regions. It is no wonder that raising babies on dry heat with heating pads or light bulbs will cause problems. Brooder designs that contain higher humidity levels are discussed in any handbook on raising babies.

Food Temperature

Food should be heated to between 100 to 106°F (38–41°C).

Many people advocate the use of the microwave for heating food; however, this method can be dangerous. Hot spots can occur within the batch of formula, and, if the formula is not thoroughly mixed, these hot spots can result in a burn of the crop lining. If you do use your microwave to warm food, be sure to mix it very thoroughly and test it with a thermometer before feeding it.

A safer way to heat food is to place the heat tolerant food container in a pan of boiling water. Once warmed, the food container can remain sitting in the warm water, which will help to keep it warm longer, particularly if a number of babies must be fed. Do make sure to check the temperature of the food again before feeding to make sure it has not become too warm while sitting in the water.

Many of the commercially prepared formulas are already precooked, and can be mixed up fresh each time. For these formulas, water from your hot water tap is warm enough.

Moisture Content

Research work done by Grau and Roudybush at the University of California determined that the ratio of solids-to-water requirements of cockatiel chicks varies with age. The moisture content of food fed to chicks less than three days of age should be 5 to 6.7 percent solids, 93.3 to 95 percent water. Chicks from four days to weaning did well on diets consisting of 20 to 25 percent solids.

This important research work was instrumental in aiding many aviculturists in diet formulation, because it helped explain why certain diets resulted in dehydration in very young chicks, and why some diets were too thin and passed through the crop too quickly in older birds.

The ratio of solids-to-water requirements of chicks varies with age.

The first feeding of the day should pass through faster than the rest of the feedings. The time required for the food to move through the crop should be 11/2 hours if the bird is less than three days of age, and up to four hours when sufficient solids are present. If from two weeks to weaning an overly dilute diet is fed, crop emptying slows, the crop becomes flaccid and voluminous, and growth rate decreases. In young chicks, sudden death can occur if solid levels are too high, with no signs of distress before death.

One way to assess the moisture content of the feed is to examine the droppings; if the feces are too well formed, the diet is too dry, and vice versa. If the diet is too dilute, the feces may turn from light green to dark green to black, with the volume of stool decreasing.

Viscosity

The same researchers also discovered that the viscosity of the diet is also very important. The diet should be of the same viscosity as yogurt, thin applesauce, or soft ice cream. If the diet is too thick, it can be difficult to empty the crop; if too thin, the diet will flow through too quickly, not providing adequate time for digestion.

Diet separation can occur if the diet is not cooked or formulated properly, so that the solid portion of the diet settles out and the liquid portion is absorbed. As the liquid is extracted from the food, the solid deposits are left behind. These deposits can ferment, curdle, and harden, leading to "sour crop." The consistency of the diet will vary somewhat, depending on the food ingredients and the method of feeding. Foods fed directly into the crop via syringe and tube need, of necessity, to be slightly thinner than foods that are spoon-fed. What is most important is that the food does not settle out if allowed to stand for any length of time.

Protein Requirements

Except for cockatiels, where the percentage of protein required in the diet for optimum growth is known, the percent protein required by most species of parrots remains an area of active research.

In cockatiels, protein levels of less than 20 percent dry weight result in slowed growth. If the protein levels are below 10 to 15 percent, poor featheration, poor growth, and stunting can occur. A globose appearance of the head and a slender beak have been shown to be indicative of metabolic bone disease, or of protein deficiency at a young age.

Rosemary Low, a well-known aviculturist, has a theory regarding protein levels; she postulates that the protein level required in the diet of each species is dependent to some extent on the growth rate of the species involved. So, for example, cockatiels that spend four weeks in the nest and have been shown to require 20 percent protein may differ from Amazons and conures, which spend eight weeks in the nest and may therefore need lower levels of protein. Whether or not her theory is correct is uncertain, but it may explain why varying levels of protein are used in various hand-feeding diets with greater or lesser success depending on the species that is being raised.

Fat Requirements

Fat requirements in the diet of neonatal psittacines is also unknown, but a few observations should be mentioned. Howard Voren and Rick Jordan, two well-recognized aviculturists and authors of the book Parrots: Hand-feeding and Nursery Management (see Useful Literature and Addresses, page 00) have stated that they feel fat level is an important aspect of diet formulation. In their experience, macaws and conures appear to do better on diets of 10 to15 percent fat, whereas cockatiels and cockatoos appear to do well on diets of 3 to 5 percent fat. Whether the fat is required to provide higher energy levels during the rapid growth phase in these species, or whether the

increase in fat compensates for some dietary deficiency, is unknown at this time.

How to Hand-feed

Different breeders use different methods of hand-feeding. For example, Rosemary Low and Matthew Vriends prefer to use a spoon. Other breeders prefer to insert a feeding tube directly into the crop; this allows them to feed large numbers of babies in a short time period. My personal preference is the use of syringes. Each bird can be assigned its own syringe, which can be sterilized and kept in its own container of disinfectant. It is easier to control the flow of food out of the syringe, and much easier to measure exactly how much food has been given. It also allows people feeding multiple birds to fill each clean syringe once from the main food container, thus preventing "double-dipping" into the main food source, which is a well-recognized route of disease spread between babies. Older, larger birds may need to be assigned two or three syringes each in order to avoid "double-dipping" because of the large volume they consume per feeding. Nonetheless, the investment in extra syringes is well worth it to prevent the spread of disease.

Despite the implement used, the basic method of hand-feeding is the same for all species. Place the baby on a flat, roughened surface with its legs squarely under it so that the bird can get some grip. Stretch the neck upwards, and hold the head from behind, just underneath and at the back of the lower jaw. Rest the syringe or spoon on the lower jaw, angling it from the left side of the beak to toward the right side. This is very important because the esophagus runs down the right side of the neck, and angling the syringe this way helps to prevent aspiration of food into the trachea, which runs down the center of the neck. Touching the syringe to the beak should have elicited the feeding response, so that the bird begins to make a vigorous pumping action with its head. This behavior is very important, because this action tends to close off the trachea even more, so that food moves down the esophagus. If, after being fed, some food remains in the mouth, or if the pumping action does not occur, gently squeezing the angle of the beak, or gently rubbing the back edges of the upper mandible, should stimulate the feeding response, causing the bird to swallow and empty its mouth. Very young chicks may not show much of a feeding response in the first few days, depending on their level of strength, so extreme care must be taken to avoid aspiration. Feeding response also varies with species; cockatoos have a very strong feeding response, whereas the feeding response in Eclectus parrots is much weaker.

When to Feed

In the first week, chicks should be fed every two hours from 6 a.m. until 11 p.m. Most breeders also check the babies once during the night and feed at 3 a.m. Studies have shown that female birds in the nest do feed throughout the night in the first few days. After the first week, the 3 a.m. feeding is moved to 4 a.m., then to 5 a.m., and so on and the daytime feedings are spread further apart, so that most birds are fed four or five times a day until out of the brooder, then three times a day until the time of

Place the baby on a flat, roughened surface with its legs squarely under it so it can get some grip.

weaning. This schedule applies to most of the larger species; species that weigh under 4 grams at birth and smaller species may require more frequent feedings, especially in the first week or so.

It is important to avoid feeding if there is still food in the crop. Noting when the crop is empty will also help you to judge if your feeding schedule is correct for that species. If food remains in the crop for several feedings, or if a large volume of food is still present in the crop by the time of the next feeding, a problem may be occurring. Keeping track of your feeding volumes and times by writing them down (especially in those early days of sleep deprivation) will make it easier to assess whether your perceptions are correct.

It is interesting to note that single babies do fuss more than when three or four siblings are kept together. However, because of the value of each individual parrot, most birds are now raised individually for

the first five days so that their feces can be monitored separately from their clutch mates. After five days of age, if development is progressing normally, brooding with clutch mates is considered beneficial.

Amount to Feed

It is important not to overfeed in the first few days to prevent aspiration of the liquidy diet, leading to aspiration pneumonia. For example, a newly hatched Amazon should only be fed 1/4 mL for the first few feedings. In the first week, the amount fed should clear the crop easily in two hours.

The second week of life is a time of very fast growth; it is just as important not to underfeed in the second week as it is not to overfeed in the first week. After that, the amount fed should clear the crop in three to three-and-a-half hours. Particularly in the first week of life, it is better to feed smaller amounts more frequently than to overload the crop, increasing the risk of aspiration and pendulous crop.

One of the more common errors people make in hand-feeding is to overfeed, particularly in species such as macaws and rose-breasted cockatoos, and in many older babies. Unfortunately, there is no hard-and-fast rule that can be applied, because the amount given varies with age, species, weight, and crop capacity. For example, as

Young macaw chicks should be fed slowly. Be careful not to overfill the crop.

a rough guideline, macaws and cockatoos should be fed roughly 10 mL per feeding at seven days; Amazons should be fed 7 mL at seven days. By the time of weaning, a large macaw may have a crop capacity of 4 ounces (120 mL), and an Amazon one of 2 ounces (60 mL). Obviously, the amount to feed increases by a few milliliters or more every few feedings. This is where consulting with other successful breeders of the same species can be helpful in judging the amount to feed your bird.

A general guideline that can be used is that the crop should feel taut to the touch, but that food should not be visible more than one third of the way up the esophagus between the crop and the lower mandible. Remember, it is better to feed a slightly smaller amount more frequently than to overload the crop. Nonetheless, between the second and third week it is important to be sure to fill the crop to capacity to accommodate for this phase of rapid growth. After that, the "less-more-often" caution applies once again.

Weight Gain

Weight gain is a valuable tool in the assessment of a baby bird's progress. The best investment anyone can make who is hand-raising babies is to purchase a good quality electronic weigh scale, and to weigh

and record the weight of each baby each day. Until the time of weaning, some weight gain should be noted every day. Baby birds should double their hatch weight by five days, and should gain weight rapidly between five days and two weeks. If weight gain slows, or if any weight loss is seen, a problem is probably present and should be investigated. Problems can include too dilute a diet, too low a protein level, underfeeding, or disease, including digestive disturbances or more serious viral diseases. A failure to gain weight is often the first and only indication of a problem, and catching the problem early is the best way to correct the situation before it becomes critical.

Remember that weight gain is only part of the answer; more essential is if the parrot is a good weight for its size. In very young chicks, the toes should be plump,

Chicks should be weighed daily and a record of their growth should be kept.

pink, and fleshy, as should the "elbows." The breast should be plump and well rounded, so that it looks like a "U" rather than a "V." If the keelbone is prominent, the bird is definitely underweight. By the same token, a baby that is too fat is also not healthy, in that it may develop liver or kidney disease. There should not be bulges of fat visible under the skin, over the hips, or on the abdomen.

When weighing your bird each day, be sure to examine it physically, as well, in order to assess these parameters.

Weaning

As if the hand-feeding process were not difficult enough, the process of weaning a bird to solid food can be even more challenging. It requires patience, careful observation, and, in some cases, a certain amount of "tough love."

Most types of parrots begin the weaning process between four to eight weeks of age. This is the age where they begin to recognize, and show interest in, dark spots against a light background. This means they will begin to attempt to pick up small objects they see placed on the ground before them.

This is the time to begin to introduce them to small, easily digested bits of food that are placed on the ground before them. Soft food diet, corn, softened whole wheat bread,

and softened pelleted food are all good choices to stimulate self-feeding behavior. Later, when the bird's beak dexterity improves, soaked and sprouted seed, cheese, or spray millet can be added. Needless to say, these bits of food will quickly be trampled and soiled with feces, so it is important to change the bedding frequently to prevent soiled bits of food from being ingested. Remember to clean the baby's feet at the same time.

As soon as a baby begins to feed on its own it is important to offer readily available fresh water. Babies love to hold objects in their beaks, so this is the perfect time to introduce a gravity-type water bottle. Babies find the little ball valve in the tip fascinating, and quickly learn they can obtain water by moving it with their beaks. Water bottles are far easier to maintain than water bowls, and there will be fewer floods! Remember to dismantle, clean, and sterilize the bottle and spout daily to prevent this object from forming a source of pathogenic bacteria.

The best kind of bedding at this time is ink-free newsprint or disposable diapers. Corncobs, walnut shells, or shavings should be avoided, because all three of these substrates have been shown to cause gizzard impactions. A glass or plastic aquarium makes an ideal cage at this time because it is easier to monitor and to clean than other cage designs.

Aside from "dot recognition," there will be other signs the bird will exhibit that will indicate that the time to wean is approaching. The bird will begin to struggle during feeding, and often scream, kick, and generally make a fuss. If allowed, most birds will refuse one or two meals, then be ready to eat again when they find they are hungry. Because you will have already begun to offer them food from the floor of the cage, let them forgo a meal or two if they wish and provide them with more tidbits to eat from the floor. Before offering each hand-feeding, check for the presence of food in the crop. If the bird has begun to eat enough from the floor to fill the crop one-third full, you can begin to decrease the amount offered per feeding, so that you don't fill the crop more than three-quarters full. Continue to gradually decrease the amount fed per meal, provided the bird is not losing too much weight. Finally, cut out the lunchtime meal first, then the breakfast meal, and then dinner.

Tom Roudybush believes that weaning is a developmental and not a learned process. He feels that delayed weaning is often caused by poor growth due to underfeeding or malnutrition, and that a slightly longer weaning period is not a cause for concern.

Nonetheless, a problem that I see frequently in my practice are birds that are still being hand-fed far past the normal age of weaning. This

Weaning is a developmental and not a learned process.

occurs because owners do not catch on to the typical weaning signals and continue to force-feed the baby until the baby loses the desire to fend for itself and becomes dependent on the hand-feeding. Once this occurs, weaning becomes far more difficult. One way to start to break this cycle is to offer warm food in a dish, and hold the dish up in front of the bird until it begins to show the feeding response. As soon as it shows the feeding response, lower the dish to the floor and leave the bird to eat on its own. It is important to leave it for a little while, or your presence will distract the bird and stimulate it to continue to beg. Continue to do this during the day, but if by evening the bird is still begging and has an empty crop, do feed it, although you should be gradually decreasing the amount of feeding per meal.

Several things should occur during the normal weaning process. The crop should shrink down to the

Weaning is considered complete when a bird is able to eat enough to maintain its own body weight for at least three consecutive days.

size that is normal for an adult bird of that species. The bird should also learn to eat enough on its own to sustain it for a 24-hour period. The bird will also undergo a process known as "pre-flight weight loss," where it may experience a 10 percent loss of body weight in preparation for leaving the nest and flight. Throughout the weaning process the bird should remain bright, alert, and active. Stools should be light in color, plentiful, and moist.

Weight loss of greater than 10 percent, stools that are dry, dark green in color, or few in number, lethargy, continued begging, or a crop that is swollen or does not empty in the expected time frame, are all signs of a problem and should be brought to the attention of your avian veterinarian.

In general, cockatiels can be weaned in about two weeks from the "dot recognition" phase, whereas species such as cockatoos can take at least six weeks if not longer. Weaning is considered completed if the bird is able to eat enough to maintain its own body weight for at least three consecutive days.

Chapter 17

Diet and Neonatal Diseases

Because this is a book on nutrition, it will be limited to diseases that are directly related to feeding. It should be noted, however, that this is in no way a complete discussion of the diseases of neonates; information of that type is available in the reference books listed in Useful Literature and Addresses, page 176.

Aspiration Pneumonia

When a bird inhales formula or fluid it is said to have aspirated. Aspiration occurs when food or fluid backs up in the mouth and covers the trachea while the bird is trying to inhale, so that fluid is then drawn into the lungs. This can occur during hand-feeding if proper care is not taken in the volume of food delivered, or if a proper feeding response has not been elicited when feeding. Occasionally it may occur after hand-feeding if the crop is too full; the bird is

placed back in its bedding, resting on it overly-full crop, and some of the food refluxes back up the esophagus into the oropharynx from where it is aspirated.

If a bird has only aspirated a small amount of formula or fluid into the trachea, it will cough, sneeze, shake its head, and gasp for breath, and fluid may be seen in the nostrils. The chick usually recovers after the coughing stops. However, if the bird has aspirated the fluid into the lung, or is unable to clear the fluid from the trachea, the bird's breathing will be labored and a clicking or rasping sound will be heard as the bird breathes. The prognosis in this case is grave; if the bird does not die immediately, pneumonia will set in, killing the bird in hours or days if not treated. Even with treatment, the chances for recovery are guarded, so aspiration is a situation best avoided.

When aspiration occurs, it is important to seek veterinary assistance immediately if there is to be any chance for survival.

Beak Deformities

There is a persistent belief in aviculture that beak deformities, specifically curved beaks, are always caused by improper hand-feeding techniques. This is not necessarily true, particularly because this defect occurs even with experienced hand-feeders who have raised many clutches without abnormalities. In some cases it is more likely that some damage has occurred to the growth plate of the beak, or to the bones of the skull themselves, altering the shearing forces that would normally keep the beak wear even. This damage may even occur due to some problem during incubation, or due to some dietary deficiency. In some cases where the injury is caused by trauma to the beak tissue, the site of damage may be so small that it is not noticed when it first occurs.

As the beak hardens, deformities become more difficult to correct.

Whatever the cause, when caught early, particularly in the first few days or weeks, these deformities may often be corrected by gently manipulating the beak several times a day to the proper configuration. In some cases various "braces" and other supports have been devised, although these are challenging to apply and maintain because they loosen and fall off every few days.

The key to correcting beak deformities lies in catching the problem early and working with the beak while it is still malleable. Later, as the beak hardens, these deformities become more difficult to correct and will need veterinary intervention. Even then, not all of these curvatures can be corrected.

Pendulous Crop

Pendulous crop occurs when the crop has been stretched beyond its natural elastic limits. It is a common result of overfeeding, particularly in two- to four-week-old macaws, white-crowned pionus, and Queen of Bavarian conures. Once the crop loses its elastic tone, food tends to sit in the crop for prolonged periods, resulting in sour crop and other digestive disorders.

If the crop has just been stretched a little by two or three overzealous feedings, such that it is beginning to hang down when the bird stands upright, decreasing the

amount fed for the next three or four feedings may correct the problem. However, if the crop has been very stretched, it will be necessary to fashion what Dr. Susan Clubb from the Avicultural Breeding Research Institute has dubbed a "crop bra." A "crop bra" is a piece of material, such as a piece of surgical stockinette, that has been fashioned into a support for the crop to lift it up into the correct position to aid it in emptying. In severe cases, or if the first two approaches are unsuccessful, a surgical approach may be necessary where part of the stretched crop wall is removed—a "tummy-tuck," so to speak.

Crop Burns

Crop burns occur when the delicate tissue of the crop, esophagus, and the tissue covering them, are damaged by thermal trauma from food that is fed too hot. It is a painful, occasionally fatal, injury that is difficult to repair. What is worse is that the injury is entirely preventable if proper care is taken.

The correct temperature of food for hand-feeding birds is between 100 and 106°F (38–41°C). Food even a few degrees higher than this can cause crop burns, as can hot spots in food that has been microwaved and not thoroughly mixed. The severity of the damage will depend on the volume of hot food ingested, as well as the tem-perature of the food. Mild crop burns may only result in damage to the internal crop lining, resulting in a crop more predisposed to secondary bacterial or fungal infection, but not visibly damaged from the outside. Severe crop burns may be seen in minutes or in days, with reddening of the skin, shock, blistering, or scabs that pull away to reveal a perforation extending from the crop through the skin layers.

Mild cases may resolve on their own as the tissues heal and scar, but more severe cases will require surgical repair. If the area of the burn is well circumscribed and not too large, repair is relatively easy in skilled hands; however, if the area of tissue damage extends over a large area of the crop or

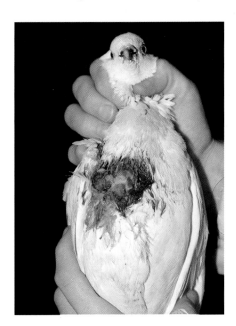

Crop burns are the result of thermal trauma from feeding food which is too hot.

165

esophagus, repair is much more difficult. In most cases, enough tissue remains to reconstruct a viable esophagus, but occasionally the damage is so extensive that no esophagus or crop can be reconstructed, and euthanasia must be considered.

For this reason, prevention is of prime importance. It is essential to invest in a good quality aquarium or cooking thermometer, because your sense of touch is not accurate enough to judge the food's temperature. Notice I stressed good quality thermometer; inexpensive microwave or meat thermometers are not accurate enough for this crucial task, and the added expense of a good thermometer is far less than the cost of veterinary intervention in this preventable condition.

If you suspect a thermal injury has occurred, or if you see evidence of scabbing or inexplicable food on the chest wall, consult with your avian veterinarian to decide how to proceed. In some cases it may be necessary to wait a few days for the original swelling to come down to see the full extent of the damage before a surgical repair is even possible.

Punctured Crop or Esophagus

Crop or esophageal punctures can occur for several reasons. First, the tissues of baby birds are extremely delicate, especially in the first few days. Feeding implements that have rough edges or are forced into the mouth can damage these delicate tissues. Second, the vigor of the feeding response may catch some hand-feeders off guard. The bird often lunges onto the syringe with such force that it almost causes the injury itself.

Signs of a crop puncture include swelling and inflammation of the tissues around the site of injury, or, in severe cases, the absence of food in the crop when the food has just been fed.

If the puncture or damage is mild, flushing the area, antibiotic therapy, and a few days of professional gavage feeding into the crop may be sufficient to allow the tissues to heal. However, if the injury is severe and food has been delivered under the skin instead of into the crop, the prognosis is guarded, and the situation will require surgical intervention.

Digestive Disturbances

The normal bacterial flora of neonatal psittacines consists of gram positive organisms. Chief among these are Lactobacillus, Staph. epidermis, Streptococcus sp., Corynebacterium sp., and Bacillus sp. Abnormal flora commonly associated with disease includes E. coli, Klebsiella, and Pseudomonas.

Gram negative bacterial infections, often accompanied by candidiasis, are the most common disorder of neonatal psittacines. Bacterial infections in the parents, especially pharyngeal or crop infections, can be transmitted to the young when feeding. In hand-feeding, the formula fed to the bird automatically contains bacteria that begin to reproduce immediately upon being warmed. Other sources of gram negative organisms include fruit, vegetables, and soft foods that have been left in the cage too long, allowing bacterial multiplication. Pseudo-monas have been collected from watering systems, especially those using polyvinyl chloride pipes. Running the water first for a few minutes before using it will help flush some of these organisms out of the system. Maintaining clean, dry, properly disinfected environments is the best way to avoid gram negative bacterial organism buildup.

One point that must be emphasized is to avoid the use of periodic prophylactic antibiotics as a preventive for bacterial infections. This practice can lead to the development of resistance in the more common bacteria, and subsequently makes them more difficult to eradicate should a serious disease outbreak occur. It also tends to wipe out the normal bacterial flora, predisposing the bird to candidiasis.

Candidiasis

Candidiasis has already been discussed in the chapter Diet and Disease, so we will only touch on it briefly here. Candidiasis is a common problem in baby birds. Preventive measures for this disease include maintaining a clean, dry, properly disinfected environment and monitoring food sources for contamination. For example, reheated formula, soft foods, sprouts, and corn are common sources. If your birds are parent-fed when first hatched before hand-feeding begins, and candidiasis appears to be more common in certain nests, then monitoring or treating the parental stock before the breeding season is warranted.

Sour Crop

Sour crop refers to the buildup of sour food in the crop. The problem with sour crop is that it is a self-perpetuating problem; sour food in the crop slows food passage, and the longer the food stays in the crop, the more sour it becomes.

Improper food preparation may lead to sour food being fed, but the most common cause these days is not allowing the crop to empty completely at least once in a 24-hour period, so that old food tends to remain in the crop and begins to sour.

Slow gut transit time is the inevitable result of sour crop, and if not resolved, total gut stasis will occur, leading to the death of the chick.

Slow Gut Transit Time

Slow gut transit time manifests itself as a crop that empties slowly, but really indicates a "slowdown" of the entire digestive tract. Dietary causes include food too cold, food too thick with inadequate moisture content, food too high in fat or protein, sour crop, and a lack of crop tone due to overstretching of the crop. An impacted foreign body, such as bedding material, may also be involved. Too hot or too cold an environmental temperature can also have this effect.

Even once the inciting cause has been determined and corrected, it is still necessary to speed the passage of food through the digestive tract until normal motility has been reestablished. Aviculturists have devised several techniques that can be employed, depending somewhat on the initiating cause.

Because any food that remains in the crop begins to sour, it is important to empty the sour food from the crop so that it does not contribute further to gut stasis. The crop is filled with warm water, massaged gently to break up any lumps of food, and emptied with a gavage tube, taking care not to damage the crop lining by puncture or by excessive suction of the delicate tissue. This rinsing procedure should be repeated several times until the fluid drawn from the crop is clear. Subcutaneous (under the skin) or interosseus (into the bone) fluids and antibiotics should also be administered. The next one or two feedings should consist of a normal volume of a balanced electrolyte solution, such as Pedialyte, or oatmeal, applesauce, and bananas baby food diluted half and half with water. If this flows through, a normal volume of dilute formula can be given for two or three feedings until normal crop motility returns. If crop motility does not return immediately, the rinsing procedure may need to be repeated for a few feedings until the tissues heal.

Slowed gut transit time must be noted and acted upon quickly if tragedy is to be avoided. A chick with marked slow gut transit time or with gut stasis is in a state of disease, dehydration, and possible starvation. Immediate veterinary intervention is often required for a successful outcome.

Diarrhea

It is difficult to describe the appearance of the feces fully, because they will vary somewhat depending on the type of hand-feeding formula being used. Normal stools do not have a foul odor. They can be any shade of tan, light brown, or light green (depending on the formula used), and should be the consistency of oatmeal or Pablum. A foul odor, or the appearance of red or black feces, can be a sign of a serious bacterial or fungal infection, and requires immediate veterinary intervention.

Constipation

True constipation is rare; however it can occur in cases of dehydration, when the food does not contain adequate moisture, or when an intestinal blockage has occurred.

If feces are being produced but appear drier and harder than normal, check the diet formulation for adequate moisture, make sure that the environmental humidity levels are adequate, and administer fluids orally or subcutaneously with the aid of your avian veterinarian to reestablish adequate hydration.

If there are no feces being produced, check the vent area to make sure feces have not caked over the opening of the vent, thereby preventing feces from being passed. If the vent is clogged, wash the vent area with a warm moistened tissue or swab, taking care not to damage the delicate tissue. If an obvious obstruction to the vent is not evident and there are no feces being produced, consult with your avian veterinarian immediately. An intestinal blockage may be present, which

is a life-threatening condition requiring immediate intervention.

Splayed Legs

Splayed legs occur most commonly as a result of malnutrition, although improper bedding can also be a cause. The most common dietary cause is calcium deficiency, though other nutrients may also be involved, including vitamin D3, phosphorus, manganese, choline, and biotin.

If caught early, many of these deformities can be corrected with proper supplementation and with taping the legs into the correct position. Because growth is rapid, many problems can be corrected in a few days to weeks if caught early.

The key to correcting these problems is speedy intervention; in cases where breeders have delayed seeking treatment for this condition until the bird is several weeks old, the damage is too far advanced and surgical manipulation, including fracturing and resetting the bone, must be attempted. In some cases, amputation of a badly affected limb (or euthanasia if both limbs are involved) must be considered.

Feather Problems

Feathers are the external manifestation of the bird's internal condition, so it is not surprising that

many dietary deficiencies result in feather abnormalities. Signs of deficiency include abnormal feather coloration, stress marks, and deformed feathers.

Abnormal feather coloration is believed to be related to a deficiency of vitamin A, riboflavin, or choline in the hand-feeding diet, although other nutritional deficiencies that have not yet been recognized may be involved. In green birds, yellow feathers may be seen,

whereas in gray birds, red or pink feathers may appear. Red birds may develop orange feathers, and some birds may develop feathers lacking any pigmentation so that they appear white.

Stress marks refer to the presence of full lines of black or other discoloration across the entire width of the feather. The bars vary in width depending on how long the "stress" situation that caused them was present. Stress factors include nutritional deficiencies or malnutrition, but may also indicate periods of environmental temperature fluctuation or any illness that was present during the development of the feather.

Abnormal feather coloration and stress marks in feathers usually disappear in the first major molt, and are seldom a cause for alarm unless other obvious signs of malnutrition are present. Deformed feathers may also be seen in Psittacine Beak and Feather Disease and in disease caused by polyomavirus. Because these viruses are highly contagious and almost always fatal, it is important to immediately isolate any bird showing abnormally formed feathers and to consult with your avian veterinarian. Any clutch mates of the affected bird, the parental breeding stock, and any other birds in the vicinity of these birds, should also be isolated immediately in an attempt to halt the spread of these two diseases, although this may be extremely difficult.

Malnutrition

Malnutrition is the end result of any dietary deficiency, whether it be caused by an inadequate hand-feeding formula, insufficient food intake, or malabsorption caused by disease.

Signs of malnutrition include a thin, bony appearance, a misshapen, enlarged head, long, thin legs and wings, late feathering, and various digestive disturbances including slow gut transit time.

For those with a great deal of experience in hand-raising, the signs of malnutrition are fairly obvious and easily recognized. For those without previous experience, early warning signs may be missed. For this reason it is wise to spend some time with an experienced, successful aviculturist who is raising the species you are interested in breeding, so that you can get a good feel of what is "normal" before attempting hand-raising yourself. This advice also applies to experienced aviculturists who are working with a new species. There is no substitute for a good look at "normal" for different species and age groups to help you get a good feel of how you are doing in comparison.

If several birds in a nursery are showing signs of malnutrition, a thorough review of the diet and of the various feeding practices used is in order.

Disease Prevention

Disease management can never be as successful as disease prevention. Although we still have much to learn, it is clear that a good quality formula and proper feeding practices are essential in the development of a healthy chick and a healthy immune system. The second essential ingredient to disease prevention is cleanliness in food management.

Food should be made up fresh for each feeding and should never be rewarmed. Countertops should be disinfected and hands should be washed thoroughly between feeding each chick. Babies should never remain sitting in soiled or wet bedding. The chance of disease being spread from one bird to another when a group of babies are being hand-fed should be minimized by feeding from youngest to oldest, and by feeding sick birds last and separately.

Any precaution you can take in how you handle your food, the environment, and the cleanliness of the brooder will go a long way in disease prevention.

Chapter 18
Hand-feeding Formulas

Commercial Diets

Although there are a number of hand-feeding formulas currently on the market, there is a concern among many aviculturists that their babies do not seem to do as well on these formulas as on the more traditional monkey biscuit-based formulas. Some manufacturers argue that these claims are unfounded, and claim to have raised many healthy babies on their formulas themselves. My own opinion lies somewhere between these two extremes. I do believe that we do not know enough yet to be sure that the rations we have formulated are completely balanced. Even if they are, what may be a balanced diet for one species may not meet all the nutritional requirements of another species. On the other hand, the development of a good hand-feeding formula would be of great benefit to most aviculturists, and would certainly take the guess-work out of diet formulation. The following is a list of several companies that have developed hand-feeding formulas that are currently on the market.

• Avi-Sci, Inc., P.O. Box 598, Okemos, Michigan 48805. Tel. (800) 942-3438.
• Harrison's Bird Diets, Inc., 5770 Lake Worth Road, Lake Worth, Florida 33463. Tel. (402) 852-2667.
• Kaytee Products, Inc., 292 E. Grand, Chilton, Wisconsin 53014. Tel. (800) 669-9580.
• Lafeber Co., R.R. #2, Odell, Illinois 60460. Tel. (800) 842-6445.
• L/M Animal Farms, Pleasant Plain, Ohio 45162. Tel. (800) 354-0407.
• Marion Zoological, 113 N. First, P.O. Box 212, Marion, Kansas 66861. Tel. (800) 327-7974.
• Pretty Bird International, Inc., 5810 Stacy Trail, Stacy, Minnesota, 55079. Tel. (800) 356-5020.
• Rolf C. Hagen (USA) Corp., Mansfield, Massachusetts 02048.
• Roudybush Inc., Box 908, Templeton, California 93465. Tel. (800) 326-1726.

Monkey Biscuit-based Formulas

A number of these formulas have been developed over the years by various aviculturists, and each varies a little depending on the species being raised.

Please keep in mind that these formulas should only be regarded as general examples. It is essential to verify that the formula you wish to use is proven for your particular species. For example, Formula Two may be too low in fat for macaws, causing stunting. For any formula, pay particular attention to the calcium:phosphorous ratio, the level of vitamin D_3, and the levels of fat and protein.

Formula One

This formula contains approximately 13 percent fat, and is used by Howard Voren and Rick Jordan for South American species. (Parrots: Handfeeding and Nursery Management, H. Voren and R. Jordan, Silvio Mattacchione & Co., 1992.)

Ingredients:

50 ZuPreem monkey biscuits
1 tablespoon wheat grass powder
1 tablespoon sunflower oil
1/2 cup hulled sunflower seed
5 cups distilled water

Directions:

All the ingredients are blenderized until smooth. The mixture is then placed into a microwave-safe bowl and covered with 1/8 inch (3mm) of water. The mixture is cooked on high until boiling, making sure that the entire mixture is heated through. The mixture is then removed from the oven, and ice cubes or water are added to bring the mixture to the proper temperature and consistency. Just before serving, a pinch of an avian vitamin supplement is added. Wheat grass powder is available from Top Flyte Organic Supplements Inc., P.O. Box 512, Pickering, Ontario, Canada L1V 2R7. Tel. (416) 831-1373.

Obviously this quantity will feed a number of birds, so the amounts used should be scaled down to suit your own needs, or the mixture can be frozen in ice cube trays and thawed as needed. Remember that many mixtures will thicken over time or during storage, so be sure to adjust to the correct consistency just before serving. Do not store this mixture in the refrigerator and reheat it, and do make sure to stir the mix well to avoid any "hot spots" in the food caused by microwaving.

This formula can be adjusted for birds that do better on a lower fat diet by eliminating the sunflower oil and using only 1/4 cup of the hulled sunflower seeds.

Formula Two

This is a basic formula that has been used for most psittacine species currently raised in captivity. (Parrots: Handfeeding and Nursery Management, H. Voren and R. Jordan, Silvio Mattacchione & Co., 1992.)

Ingredients:

50 ZuPreem monkey biscuits
2–4-ounce jar of strained creamed corn (baby food)
1–4-ounce jar of strained garden

vegetables (baby food)

1 heaping tablespoon of salt-free peanut butter

Directions:

Soak monkey biscuits in water until soft. Add enough water to cover the biscuits, and microwave until boiling along the edges and stir. Once heated through, remove from the oven and add all the ingredients. Blenderize the formula, and add ice cubes or water as needed until the desired temperature and consistency is reached. Just before serving, add a pinch of an avian vitamin supplement.

Formula Three

Greg Harrison recommended this recipe several years ago. It is similar to the second recipe, with some minor variations.

Ingredients:

1–4-ounce jar strained creamed corn (baby food)

1–4-ounce jar strained spinach (baby food)

30 ZuPreem monkey biscuits

3 cups water

1/2 cup cheddar cheese

Directions:

Blend all the ingredients together, and blenderize until it achieves the correct consistency. More monkey biscuits or more water can be added as needed to achieve the desired consistency. It can be frozen in individual portions, and thawed as needed.

Other Formulas

Aside from the formulas listed above, there are dozens of others that have been created and that have varying degrees of success depending on the species with which they are used. For example, Rosemary Low uses a formula that consists basically of equal parts of canned fruit cocktail and bone and beef broth with strained vegetables (baby food); the San Diego Zoo has had great success in rearing lories with a recipe that contains wheat germ, Karo syrup, and trout chow. As I have said before, the choice of formula to use is a matter of individual preference and experience. I hope these examples will give you some ideas of where to begin.

Useful Literature and Addresses

For Information on Nutrition

Bird Talk Magazine, P.O. Box 57347, Boulder, Colorado 80322-7347 Tel. (303) 786-7306

Bird World Magazine, P.O. Box 51247, Pacific Grove, California 93950 Tel. (408) 375-0417

Journal of the Association of Avian Veterinarians, 5770 Lake Worth Road, Lake Worth, Florida 33463-3299

The Pet Bird Report, 2236 Mariner Square Dr., Number 35, Alameda, California 94501

Seminars in Avian and Exotic Pet Medicine, WB Saunders Co., The Curtis Center, Independence Square West, Philadelphia, Pennsylvania 19106-3399

Watchbird Magazine, American Federation of Aviculture, P.O. Box 56218 Phoenix, Arizona 85079-6218

Clinical Avian Medicine and Surgery, 1986 Harrison, G., and Harrison, L., WB Saunders Co., Philadelphia, Pennsylvania

Complete Book of Macaws The, 1990, Rosemary Low, Barron's, Hauppauge, New York

Complete Book of Parrots, 1989, Rosemary Low, Barron's, Hauppauge, New York

For Information on Hand-feeding, Aviculture, and Pediatrics

Parrots: Handfeeding and Nursery Management, Howard Voren, Rick Jordan. Published 1992 by Silvio Mattacchione & Co. 1793 Rosebank Rd. N., Pickering, Ontario, Canada L1V 1P5. Distributed in United States and Canada by Firefly Books Ltd., 250 Sparks Ave., Willowdale, Ontario, Canada M2H 2S4

Parrot Production: Incorporating Incubation, John and Pat Stoodley, 1983, Bezels Publications, Lovedean, Portsmouth, POB OSW, England

Parrots: Their Care and Breeding, Second Edition. 1986, Rosemary Low, Blandford Press, Artillery House, Artillery Row, London, SW1P 1RT, England

Psittacine Aviculture: Perspectives, Techniques, and Research.

AviCultural Breeding and Research Center, 1471 Folsom Road, Loxahatchee, Florida 33470-4942

Pellet Manufacturers

Aviary North: Canaviax Products, 41 The Links Road, Willowdale, Ontario, Canada M2P IT7

Hagen: Rolf C. Hagen (USA), Mansfield, Maine 02048 and Montreal, Quebec H4R 188

Harrison's: HBD, Inc., 5770 Lake Worth Road, Lake Worth, Florida 33453

Lake's: Lake's Minnesota Macaws, Inc., 639 Stryker Avenue, St. Paul, Minnesota 55107

Mazuri: PMI Feeds, Inc., 1401 S. Hanley Road, St. Louis, Missouri 63144

Pretty Bird: Pretty Bird International, Inc., 5810 Stacy Trail, P.O. Box 177, Stacy, Minnesota 55079-0177

Roudybush: Roudybush Diets, Box 908, Templeton, California 93465

Topper: Topper Bird Ranch, Rt. 19, Box 529, Lexington, North Carolina 27292

Index

K, vitamin, *see* Vitamins

Legumes, 8, 61–62
Leucine, 7, 35, 49
Light,
  effects on food, 5, 9, 19, 20
  bird requirements for, 16, 17
Lipids, *see* Fats
Liver,
  diseases of, 18, 98
  functions, 8, 16, 23, 56–57, 98
  source of, 15, 37, 38, 39, 40, 42, 43, 62, 116
Lories, 1, 2, 51, 53, 55, 115–116, 122
Lorikeets, 1, 51, 53, 115–116, 122
Lovebirds, 89, 114, 151
Lysine, 7, 8, 31, 35, 36, 49, 86, 118

Macaws, 1, 2, 15, 64, 107, 119, 174
Magnesium, *see* Minerals
Malnutrition, 171
Manganese, *see* Minerals
Meats, 7, 8, 26, 61, 116
Methionine, 7, 8, 24, 29, 56, 78, 86, 98
Minerals, 5, 11, 12, 24–35, 44–45, 47–48, 140–141
  arsenic, 34
  blocks, 141–142
  bromine, 34
  calcium, 12, 16, 22, 23, 24–26, 44–45, 47, 61, 65, 86, 88–90, 115, 117, 118
  chloride, 28, 44–45, 47
  chromium, 33
  cobalt, 32, 44–45, 48
  copper, 9, 31, 44–45, 48
  excesses, 65
  fluoride, 33
  food sources of, 40–43
  iodine, 32, 44–45, 48, 96
  iron, 9, 12, 23, 27, 30, 31, 32, 44–45, 48, 57, 61, 91–92, 116
  macrominerals, 12, 24–30

magnesium, 27–28, 44–45, 47
manganese, 30, 44–45, 48
microminerals, 12, 30–34
molybdenum, 32, 34, 48
nickel, 34
phosphorus, 26–27, 44–45, 47
potassium, 28–29, 44–45, 47
selenium, 33, 44–45, 48
signs of deficiency, 44–45, 86, 88, 90, 95–96
signs of excess, 47–48, 91
silicon, 34
sodium, 28, 44–45, 47
sources of, 27, 40–43
sulfur, 29, 32, 44–45, 47
vanadium, 34
zinc, 31, 32, 44–45, 48, 93, 104
Molds, 105–106
Molting, *see* Feathers
Molybdenum, *see* Minerals
Mouth, 51
Mynahs, 55, 91, 116

Niacin, *see* Vitamins
Nose, 51
Nutrition, 4
  importance of, 3
  proper, 1
  study of, 5, 36

Obesity, 3, 6, 97, 112, 113, 117
Osteomalacia, 16, 25, 89, 114
Oxalic acid, 26
Oxidation, 6, 9, 15, 17, 23, 35, 137
Oxygen transport, 11

Pancreas, 55
Pantothenic acid, *see* Vitamins
Parsley, 106
Pellets, 6, 63–67, 69, 111, 114, 115
Pharynx, 52
Phenylalanine, 7

Phosphorus, *see* Minerals
Phytic acid, 26, 27, 31, 61
Pigeons, 53, 99, 115
Plants, 102–103
  safe, 108
  poisonous, 108
Poisons, *see* Toxins
Polyomavirus, 170
Polyuria, 95
Potassium, *see* Minerals
Poultry, 3, 4, 7, 26, 30, 33, 35, 57, 78
Preservatives, 137–138
Probiotics, 139–140
Proline, 7, 35, 49
Prostaglandins, 9, 21
Protozoal infections, 95, 99, 100
Proteins, 5, 7, 35–36, 56, 64, 78
  animal, 8, 111
  biological availability of, 7
  biological values of, 7, 8
  composed of, 7
  excess, 20, 22
  functions, 7
  importance of, 7
  lack of, 6, 19
  requirements, 111, 143
Proventriculus, 54
Psittacine beak and feather disease, 86, 118, 170
Psittacine proventricular dilation syndrome, 84, 119
Pylorus, 55
Pyroxidine, *see* Vitamins

Quarantine period, 85

Recipes,
  A.B.R.C., 122
  basic soft-bill, 123
  color food, 135
  egg food, 135
  Lory diets, 122–123
  other, 133–134
  soft food, 120–122
Regurgitation, 53, 101
Reproduction, 144–145
Riboflavin, *see* Vitamins

Photo Credits

Dr. R. Dean Axelson,
front cover, pages 2, 6,
13, 15, 35, 50, 62, 63, 68,
71, 74, 82, 84, 86, 87, 88,
91, 92, 93, 94, 96, 110,
111, 119, 120, 127, 136,
146, 157, 161, 165, 170
(bottom), 171

Dr. Rick Axelson,
pages 11, 24, 170 (top)

Dr. Louise Bauck,
pages 21, 70, 75, 112,
113, 117, 118, 124, 143,
147, 150, 162, 164

Dr. Petra Burgmann,
pages 72, 80, 97, 102

Canaviax Publications Ltd.,
inside back cover

Susan Green,
pages 16, 19, 29, 36, 76,
77, 101, 109

Mark Hagen,
pages 64, 154

B. Everett Webb,
inside front cover, pages 14,
27, 58, 59, 67, 73, 79, 103,
114, 122, 139, 149, 152,
back cover